Twenty-five years of the Archers

Twenty-five years of
THE ARCHERS

A Who's Who of Ambridge

British Broadcasting Corporation

The map on pages 6-7 was produced at the
Department of Geography, University of
Leicester. Research by David Turnock,
Cartography by Ruth Rowell.

Published by the
British Broadcasting Corporation
35 Marylebone High Street
London W1M 4AA

Written by Jock Gallagher

ISBN 0 563 17009 3

First published 1975

Reprinted 1976

Printed in England by Stevens Press Limited
Long Eaton Nottingham
(a member of the Oxley Printing Group)

Who's Who In Ambridge

The writers of BBC Radio's *The Archers* have been telling millions of listeners their everyday story of country folk every day for 25 years: and in that quarter of a century, they have peopled the mythical village of Ambridge with mythical men, women and children. They have given them names, personalities and even family-trees. They have given them houses to live in, land to own, jobs to do, and animals to tend or terrorise.

Into these paper people, the actors and actresses have breathed life. They have given them accents, grunts, sighs, laughs and the odd impediment.

Between them, the writers and the actors have transformed the figments of their own imagination into reality for millions of others. Today, when regular listeners talk about Dan, Doris or any of the villagers of Ambridge, they don't regard them simply as characters from a radio programme, they discuss them as they would any of their other friends.

In previous books, we have chronicled some of the events that have happened in the village and how they were seen through the eyes of Doris Archer. In this *Who's Who*, we look at the people themselves and this time we see them through the eyes of an independent but fascinated observer.

In the first section, we see the folk who are around the village now: some who have made their mark on the community, some who are perhaps only part of the background scenery. In the second part, we list those characters who have either died or left Ambridge to make a new life elsewhere. Together, the two sections offer a comprehensive collection of pen portraits of villagers and visitors over the past 25 years.

Ambridge

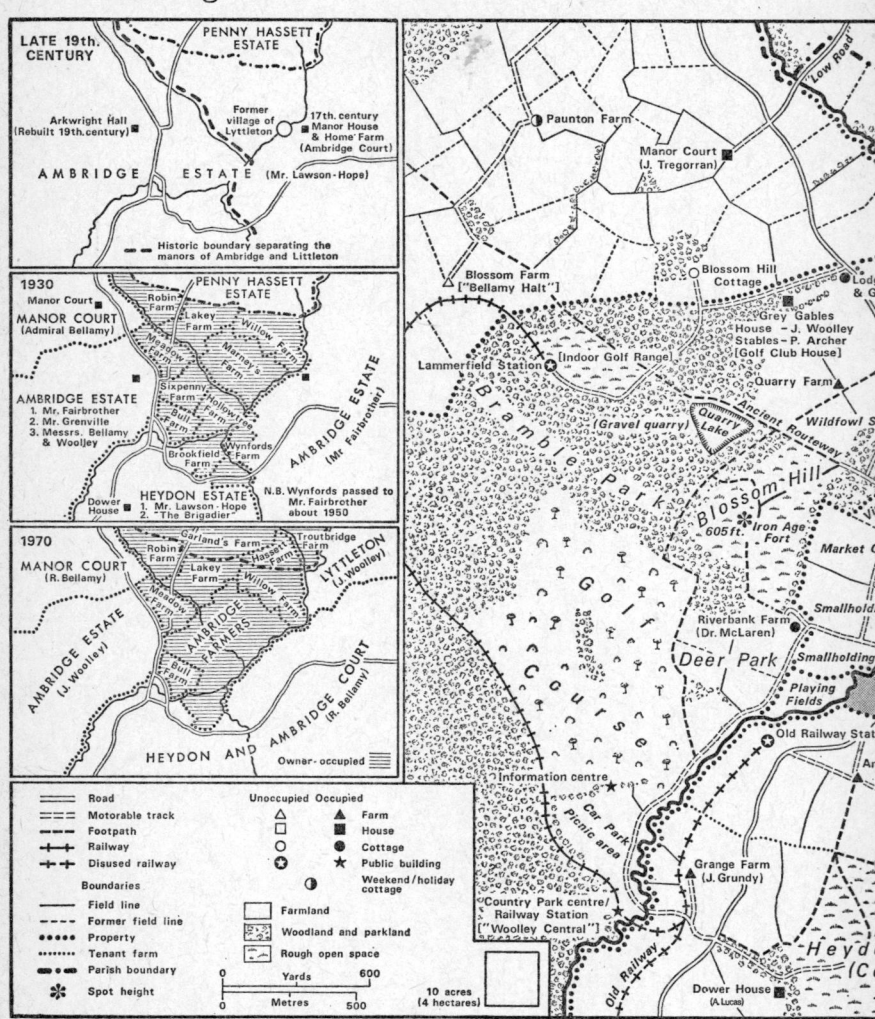

LATE 19th. CENTURY

Arkwright Hall (Rebuilt 19th. century) ■

PENNY HASSETT ESTATE

Former village of Lyttleton ○

17th. century Manor House & Home Farm (Ambridge Court) ■

AMBRIDGE ESTATE (Mr. Lawson-Hope)

– – Historic boundary separating the manors of Ambridge and Littleton

1930

Manor Court

MANOR COURT (Admiral Bellamy)

PENNY HASSETT ESTATE

Robin Farm

Lakey Farm

Willow Farm

Marney's Farm

Meadow Farm

Sixpenny Farm

Hollowtree Farm

Bull Farm

Wynfords Farm

Brookfield Farm

AMBRIDGE ESTATE

1. Mr. Fairbrother
2. Mr. Grenville
3. Messrs. Bellamy & Woolley

AMBRIDGE ESTATE (Mr Fairbrother)

Dower House

HEYDON ESTATE
1. Mr. Lawson-Hope
2. "The Brigadier"

N.B. Wynfords passed to Mr. Fairbrother about 1950

1970

MANOR COURT (R. Bellamy)

AMBRIDGE ESTATE (J. Woolley)

Garland's Farm

Robin Farm

Lakey Farm

Hassett

Willow Farm

Troutbridge Farm

LYTTLETON (J. Woolley)

AMBRIDGE FARMERS

Meadow

Bull Farm

HEYDON AND AMBRIDGE COURT (R. Bellamy)

Owner-occupied ▤

Paunton Farm

Manor Court (J. Tregorran)

Low Road

Blossom Farm ["Bellamy Halt"] △

Blossom Hill Cottage ○

Lodge & G

Grey Gables House – J. Woolley
Stables – P. Archer [Golf Club House]

Lammerfield Station

[Indoor Golf Range]

Quarry Farm

Ancient Routeway

(Gravel quarry)

Quarry Lake

Wildfowl S

BRAMBLE PARK

Blossom Hill

605 ft.

Iron Age Fort

Market G

GOLF

COURSE

Deer Park

Riverbank Farm (Dr. McLaren)

Smallhold

Smallholding

Playing Fields

Old Railway Stat

Information centre ★

Car Park Picnic area

An

Country Park centre/ Railway Station ["Woolley Central"] ★

Grange Farm (J. Grundy)

Old Railway

Heyd (C

Dower House (A. Lucas) ▤

Legend

═══	Road
= = =	Motorable track
- - -	Footpath
┿┿┿	Railway
┿ + ┿	Disused railway

Boundaries

——	Field line
– – –	Former field line
•••••	Property
········	Tenant farm
●—●—●	Parish boundary
✳	Spot height

	Unoccupied	Occupied	
Farm	△	▲	
House	□	■	
Cottage	○	●	
Public building	✪	★	
Weekend/holiday cottage	◑		

▭ Farmland

▦ Woodland and parkland

▱ Rough open space

Yards 0 — 600

Metres 0 — 500

10 acres (4 hectares)

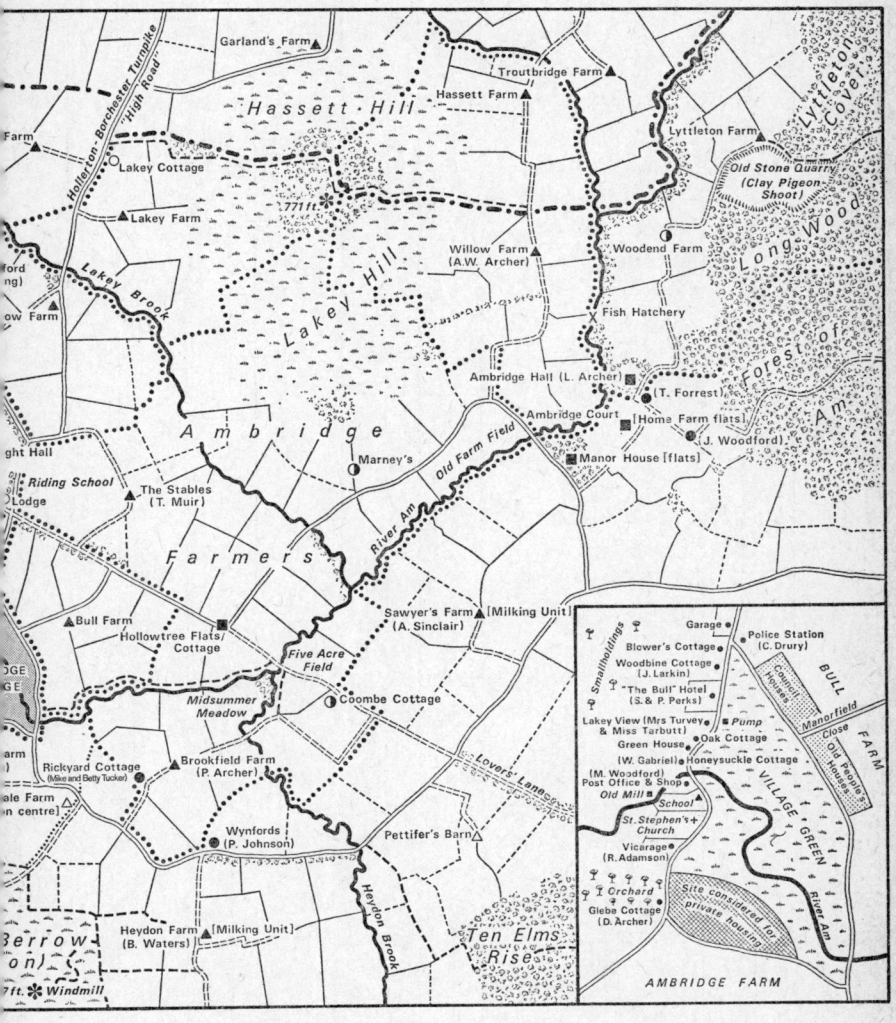

Garland's Farm ▲

Troutbridge Farm ▲

Hassett Farm ▲

Hassett·Hill

Farm

Lyttleton Farm

Lyttleton Cover

Holleron-Borchester Turnpike 'High Road'

Lakey Cottage ▲

Old Stone Quarry (Clay Pigeon-Shoot)

777 ft. ✳

▲ Lakey Farm

Long Wood

Lakey Brook

Lakey · Hill

Willow Farm (A.W. Archer) ▲

Woodend Farm ▲

Fish Hatchery

ow Farm

A m b r i d g e

Ambridge Hall (L. Archer) ▥

(T. Forrest) ▥

Ambridge Court ▥ [Home Farm flats]

(J. Woodford) ▥

Forest of Am

Marney's ○

Old Farm Field

ght Hall

▲ Riding School
Lodge

The Stables (T. Muir) ▲

River Am

Manor House [flats] ▥

F a r m e r s

▲ Bull Farm

Hollowtree Flats/ Cottage ▥

Sawyer's Farm (A. Sinclair) ▲ [Milking Unit]

Five Acre Field

DGE
GE

Midsummer Meadow

Coombe Cottage ○

Garage ○

Police Station (C. Drury) ●

Blower's Cottage ◡

Smallholdings

Woodbine Cottage (J. Larkin)

Council Houses

BULL FARM

Manorfield Close

"The Bull" Hotel (S. & P. Perks) ●

Pump ⊗

Old Peoples Houses

Lakey View (Mrs Turvey & Miss Tarbutt)

Oak Cottage ◡

Green House

arm

Rickyard Cottage (Mike and Betty Tucker) ●

▲ Brookfield Farm (P. Archer)

Lovers' Lane

(W. Gabriel) Honeysuckle Cottage

VILLAGE GREEN

ale Farm
n centre) △

(M. Woodford)
Post Office & Shop
Old Mill ■

School ■

River Am

Wynfords ● (P. Johnson)

Pettifer's Barn △

St. Stephen's Church ✚

Vicarage (R. Adamson)

Site considered for private housing

errow
on)

Heydon Farm (B. Waters) ▲ [Milking Unit]

Heydon Brook

Ten Elms Rise

Orchard ✦

Glebe Cottage (D. Archer)

7 ft. ✳ Windmill

AMBRIDGE FARM

Dorothy Adamson

Mrs Adamson, in her thirties, came to Ambridge in 1973 when her husband became the new vicar. Having been born and brought up in the suburbs of Birmingham, she at first found life in the country a bit strange, and the big, old vicarage difficult to manage while looking after two children at the same time. Now that there's a new vicarage, however – much the same as the small, modern houses she's always lived in before – she is very much happier; and having more time, she is able to get more involved in village life.

Actually she became very interested in the history of Ambridge when she found a hidden wall-safe in the old rectory which contained parish records going back to 1706. She doesn't see herself as a countrywoman just yet, but she is moving in the right direction, she says.

Richard Adamson

Before taking over as vicar in Ambridge, the Rev. Richard Adamson was in charge of a church in a very busy Birmingham suburb. The most startling change he discovered was in the style of life. In the city, people rushed around seemingly achieving very little, while the measured pace in the countryside always seemed to have purpose. But his experiences in Birmingham have proved invaluable in the village. For example, he worked with the Samaritans there, and when one of his new parishioners tried to commit suicide, he was well equipped to help. Then as a trained scout leader he was able to take over the local pack from Philip Archer, who had been running it temporarily. He was also able to add his experience as a bell-ringer to the local group led by Tom Forrest.

Outside church activities, he's also proved a welcome addition to the village. He has joined the cricket team and is a very good fast bowler.

8

Dan Archer

It's a pity the English village doesn't have – like its counterpart in some other European countries – a patriarch. If it did, the title would settle without dispute on the broad shoulders of Dan Archer, and it would accurately describe the role he plays in the tiny, rural community of Ambridge. Now in his seventies, he is the village's natural leader – loved and respected by everyone. It is to him and his wife, Doris, that most people turn in times of trouble.

Dan himself would be surprised to hear such comments and that in itself is one of his qualities. He goes about his business and his life in a quiet but firm manner, seldom deviating from a predetermined course and unaware that his every action is having an impact on the community around him. He never does anything for effect and would, therefore, not realise it was having effect.

His family links with Ambridge go back several generations and he was born and bred in the village. What formal education he had was at the local school, and when he left – at 13 – he went straight to work for his father, the tenant at Brookfield Farm.

In those unmechanised days, it was a hard life on the farm, and the fresh-faced young Dan soon learned that getting up at dawn to milk the cows was good for the soul if not for the physical comfort of a young farmer. He took to the work naturally and eagerly, and by the time he was eighteen he had filled out to be a handsome,

9

strapping young man. Two years later he needed both the physical strength and the strength of character he had built up over the years.

At the time, Dan and his brother John were serving in the army during the First World War. Dan had just finished training and was awaiting a posting to the Front, where John already was. But his father became ill, and Dan was discharged on compassionate grounds to return to run the farm. His father died soon after he got back and then his mother also died soon afterwards. Not quite 21, Dan was left to run the farm single-handed for nearly two years until John got back from the war. Their other brother Frank had already emigrated to New Zealand.

John didn't stay at Brookfield for long. The villagers still think that he left because his army experiences had unsettled him and given him wanderlust. In fact, it was a bitter personal conflict between the two brothers that led to him leaving Ambridge quietly and suddenly on Boxing Day just a year after the end of the Great War.

John had come home to a hero's welcome from the villagers and he took full advantage of the situation, particularly with the local girls. He spent more time gallivanting than working on the farm. At first Dan was understanding and didn't press his brother to help, but gradually discontent began to smoulder and it was fanned by the attention John was paying a certain young Doris Forrest. Doris was the girl that Dan had decided he wanted to marry, although he hadn't actually got round to asking her. John knew about Dan's intentions but he ignored them, and things came to a head on Christmas night when the brothers had spent the day with the Forrest family. Dan saw his brother catching Doris under the mistletoe and it was too much for him. When they got back to Brookfield, he decided to have it out with John.

Bitter words were hurled around and all Dan's frustration about John's laziness came out. It soon became clear that Brookfield wasn't big enough for both of them. One of them would have to leave. But who? The only way to settle it was physically. There and then, Christmas or no Christmas, the two shaped up to each other in the barn at Brookfield.

It was a brutal and bloody fight with neither sparing any effort to hurt the other. In the end it was the older brother, Dan, who was left standing. He was bruised and battered but John was in an even worse state, and as he lay there in the dirt, Dan made him confirm his promise that, as the loser, he would leave Brookfield and Ambridge right away. Hours later Dan got back to the farmhouse after tending the stock and his brother had gone.

It was perhaps this single incident that put the steely edge into Dan Archer's determination and gave him the courage to fight all the odds that Nature stacks against any young man trying to build up a farm. Anyway, Dan did marry Doris Forrest, who until her marriage had worked in service at the local squire's house.

That was in 1920, and they later had two sons, Jack and Philip, and a daughter Christine. All the while they were raising their family, Dan cherished a dream that he would one day own Brookfield instead of just renting it. He had to wait more than thirty years before the dream came true, but in 1954 he put every penny he had – and a lot more that he didn't have – into buying the farm and land from the squire. The day the deeds were transferred to his name was the proudest of Dan's life. Although he had long since won the respect of his neighbours, this was the moment Dan felt he had really arrived as a farmer. Every last acre was his and there was nobody at the Big House who expected the occasional tug at the forelock.

Like all farmers, Dan has had his problems. In 1956 he was forced to change his policy when foot-and-mouth disease destroyed his cattle. A year later he lost about a fifth of his potatoes through blight and in 1958

11

he lost most of his oats in a fire. The very next year he broke his leg and his anxiety to get back on the farm caused another fall in which he broke a rib and contracted pneumonia. And if that wasn't enough, 1960 brought fowl-pest and Dan abandoned poultry altogether. But luckily that was the end of a winter that had lasted more than four years.

His various crises had brought him round to thinking about getting together with other local farmers to weather the storms. In 1961 he became chairman of Ambridge Dairy Farmers Ltd, an amalgam of Brookfield and two other farms. It was one of these farms that his son Philip later took over when he joined the company.

When Dan decided to go into retirement, it was agreed that Philip would become chairman of the company, now just Ambridge Farmers Ltd and very much a family concern, and Dan and Doris would move out of Brookfield. For Dan, after a lifetime in farming, it was too much of a shock and it wasn't long before retirement became semi-retirement and he was back working at Brookfield.

Over the years, Dan would have been forgiven for concentrating on his farming and leaving the general affairs of the village to others. But he didn't. He has always been a keen church-goer and for many years he sang baritone in the choir and was chairman of the Parochial Church Council. He was also chairman of the Parish Council for many years and since 1966 he has been chairman of Ambridge Protection Society, which he helped to form to preserve the village's environment.

He is still busily involved in village life and his deeply-lined face shows every bit as much determination as it must have done fifty-five years ago when he won the right – the hard way – to be called Dan Archer of Brookfield Farm, Ambridge. He's no longer at Brookfield, but in any case he's been known for a long time as just Dan Archer of Ambridge.

David Archer

At sixteen, young David Archer does not want to follow the family tradition of going into farming. He is at boarding school studying for the A levels that he hopes will eventually gain him a university place and pave the way for a career in politics.

The younger son of Philip and Jill Archer, David is not really at ease in the country, and spends most of the school vacations in Borchester and other big towns attending political meetings and going to the libraries.

When he went to the village school, he was quite an athletic youngster who played football for the school team. But his mop of blonde hair gained him the nickname of 'Snowball' and he found this so disconcerting that he gave up soccer to try to become 'a bit more anonymous', as he put it.

He has already taken his O levels and succeeded in picking up seven – including English and History, the main subjects he will be taking at A level. He is also interested in environmental studies, and some years back he carried out a project in Ambridge on the effect of traffic on the wildlife of the district.

Doris Archer

Mrs Doris Archer matches up to most people's idea of a farmer's wife. She looks every inch the part and seeing her walking through Ambridge you know she's just come off the farm. A small, plumpish woman in her seventies, she is still spritely and always has a friendly

13

smile on her weathered face. She has about her that aura of contentment, the hallmark of the English countrywoman.

She has, of course, a lot to be contented with. Her life, though often hard, has been happy and fulfilling. She has worked alongside her husband, Dan, as they built up Brookfield Farm together. She has seen her children grow up and have families of their own and then their families have families. Now she's getting excited about the expected arrival of her fourth great-grandchild, to Tony and Pat Archer.

Mrs Archer was born and bred in Ambridge and, like so many of her generation, the only thing for her to do when she left the village school was to go into service. But she was luckier than most and managed to get into the Big House working for the squire. The vacancies there were few and far between and the alternative for Ambridge girls was to go away from home and live in somewhere.

Doris started off as a kitchen-maid and has bitter-sweet memories of those days. She can remember having to get up at the crack of dawn and walk through the driving rain to the Big House. Once there, she had to do all the donkey work before the cook would deign to prepare breakfast. It was a hard life for a thirteen-year-old girl. But she remembers, too, the thrill of seeing the landed gentry celebrating the traditional English events like harvest and Christmas: the tables laden with food, wine and ale flowing fast, the handsome men and the elegant ladies. It was a glimpse of a beautiful world . . . at least as she saw it.

It was, of course, a world that a poor country girl could never join and when Dan Archer, then a burly young tenant farmer, asked her to marry she had no hesitation. She became a farmer's wife in 1920.

It wasn't a way of life for the weak. If doing the scullery chores in service was hard, being a farmer's chief cook, bottlewasher and labourer – at a time when there were no mechanical aids on the farm – was almost as bad as doing hard labour in a chain gang. It was remorseless toil – seven days a week, fifty-two weeks a year. The livestock never recognised high days or holidays and a wife was expected to share the responsibility of tending and feeding them.

How any woman in those days found time to bring up a family is something to be marvelled at today. Dan and Doris had two sons, Jack and Philip, and a daughter, Christine (now Mrs Paul Johnson). Doris simply added the role of mother to her already long list of responsibilities, and went on with a very hectic life which, to her, seemed absolutely ordinary.

Despite the farm and the family, she always found time to be involved in the social life of the village. She shared her husband's love of singing and they used to do duets together at village socials – many of which she organised. She is a member of the Women's Institute and has really been up to her elbows in jam and Jerusalem. For many years she organised all the catering for the meetings and could always be relied upon to lead the choral singing. She tends to take things a bit more quietly now but she has by no means 'retired'.

Of all the ups and downs of her life, the two 'downs' that distressed her most were when her brother Tom was charged with murder and later when her elder son Jack had to go into a mental hospital. The murder charge against Tom was eventually dropped, but his arrest and the pre-trial publicity left Doris very shaken. The charge was made after a poacher had been killed in a shooting incident. Tom's case wasn't helped by the fact that he'd been heard threatening the man, Bob Larkin, because he'd been pestering Tom's girl-friend. In the end it was realised that the death was a tragic accident and he was cleared.

Jack's illness had started several years before that accident but his health had deteriorated very badly two years earlier and he had a breakdown which led to him

15

going into the mental hospital. His condition improved and he came home but he caused Doris and his family anxiety until his death in 1972.

An example of how perfectly Doris Archer represents the typical countrywoman was when – in 1971, her golden wedding year – the local newspaper published excerpts from her diaries over the years. It was a great success and she followed it up a year later by publishing another book, which was really the year in the life of a farmer's wife.

The book was as unpretentious as her life. It very simply traced the changing seasons, and their effects on the farming community; the relationships between members of a tiny community, and how they become inextricably involved with each other. It showed life in the country as she saw it – a sort of bird's-eye view!

Elizabeth Archer

Elizabeth Archer, David's young sister, was born with a hole-in-the-heart. But after an operation three years ago, when she was five, she is now perfectly fit and leads a normal life.

She went to the village school and later transferred to Borchester when the local school closed. She is very popular with the other children because of her gay, extrovert personality. She also goes to the Brownies and is well on her way to collecting a record number of activity badges.

Like her big sister, Shula, she loves horses but seems just as happy grooming them as Shula is jumping them.

Jill Archer

For most women, coping with a husband, four children, a large farmhouse and a clutch of hens would be more than enough to keep them busy. But Mrs Jill Archer, wife of Philip Archer, also finds time to act as company secretary to the farm business *and* serve as a local councillor. Jill is one of those indefatigable women for whom nothing seems to be too much trouble and who never seems to get flustered. Whenever the villagers have a problem – about anything from public rights-of-way to the closure of the local school – they can always be sure of help from her.

A few years back, she led a very vigorous campaign to stop the county council shutting down the school. She was partially successful, fending off the inevitable for nearly three years, but even when the school did close, she immediately set about establishing a bus service to take children from the village to their new school.

She is also active in the Women's Institute and is a former branch president.

Despite all these activities, Jill is particularly careful never to neglect her family responsibilities. Her husband's first wife was tragically killed in a fire less than six months after their wedding, and she knows this still affects him from time to time so she is more than usually understanding of his moods. Her youngest daughter, Elizabeth, was born with a hole-in-the-heart condition and needed very careful nursing until she was five and could have an operation to give her normal health. Jill has ridden such storms as though they were minor squalls and as a result now has tremendous strength of character.

Kenton Archer

Life on the ocean wave seems ideal to eighteen-year-old Kenton Archer, who left Ambridge to join the Merchant Navy two years ago.

Although he was exceptionally clever at school, Kenton was always pushed into the background by his precocious twin sister, Shula, and that may have influenced his decision to go to sea! Actually he never was very interested in farming – much to the disappointment of his father, Philip Archer – and after doing very well in science at Borchester Grammar School, he took

17

up meteorology and it was this that led to the Merchant Navy.

He joined up as a cadet and went to Southampton for his initial training. After that he went to sea for a six-month tour of duty and that, he said, was the most exciting time of his life. He sailed right up into the North Atlantic and was able to see the weather ships in operation. Stormy conditions and the long spells of duty did nothing to lessen his enthusiasm. When he recently came home on leave – in uniform for the first time – he talked almost non-stop about his experiences and, for once, out-did Shula!

Laura Archer

Although her New Zealand accent is still as jarring to the Ambridge ear as it was when she first arrived nearly twenty years ago, Mrs Laura Archer is now more or less accepted as a 'local'. Whether it's simply because of her surname and her links-through-marriage with the Archer family or the way she has thrown herself into village affairs, one cannot be quite sure.

She has been accepted well enough for her to be elected to the parish council and – perhaps more significantly – to the presidency of the village Women's Institute. At the same time, it must be said that the folk haven't swallowed her lock, stock and barrel. They still react to some of her machinations and, whenever her natural bossiness gets close to downright interference, she gets told exactly where she can go – and that's not just back to New Zealand!

Within the Archer family, she is 'Aunt Laura', being the widow of Dan Archer's brother Frank. He was very successful in New Zealand, and when he died she was left very comfortably endowed. Her money did cause a few problems when she first came to Ambridge because she was terribly obvious with it. Once people got used to her and it, however, it ceased to be a talking point.

Pat Archer

As a young farmer just starting out on his own, Tony Archer was always being told that he needed a wife. For his part, he knew exactly the kind of girl that he wanted. So when Pat Lewis, a very attractive young Welsh girl, came to Ambridge to visit her uncle, she didn't really have a chance. She was swept off her feet and she and Tony were married only months after meeting. Their first child is expected soon.

Pat, who lived in Wales with her widowed mother, first came to Ambridge for a short visit to the farm owned by her uncle, Haydn Evans, in partnership with Tony Archer. Back home she had looked after a pedigree herd of Welsh Blacks and was also experienced in general farm management. When they met, she and Tony took to each other immediately and, when she went back to Wales, he soon found an excuse to visit her there. A few weeks later she was back in Ambridge, and when her uncle slipped a disc she didn't need much persuasion to stay on to help him. It wasn't long before she accepted Tony's proposal.

After honeymooning in Tenerife, she quickly settled down to English life, and her warm, open personality has made her popular in an area that doesn't always warm to 'foreigners'. Before her pregnancy, she entered into the spirit of things when the local ladies challenged the men to a football match. She ended up captaining the ladies' side and acquitted herself well. She has also joined the committee to run the annual fête, and goes to the Women's Institute meetings. Like many farmers' wives, she has her own sideline: she keeps some free-range hens and markets her eggs through a health-food shop. She hopes to go on with that after the baby is born.

Peggy Archer

As a former licensee – and still owner – of the local pub, Mrs Peggy Archer has been at the centre of Ambridge's social life for many years. She almost perfectly fits the part of country landlady and there are few who can now remember that she is in fact 'a foreigner'.

She was born and brought up within earshot of London's famous Bow Bells and had never even been out of the city until she fell in love with Jack Archer, married him and came to settle with him in Ambridge. It was the war that brought them together. Peggy, who had left grammar school to become a dressmaker, was not quite twenty when she joined the ATS determined to do her bit for the war effort. She was the stores orderly who kitted out one particularly dashing young soldier, Jack, the eldest son of Dan and Doris Archer. Like so many wartime romances, theirs moved fast and they were married before Peggy's twenty-first birthday.

At the end of the war they came to Ambridge, where Jack had a smallholding. Peggy found the transition very difficult. Life in a tiny English village was vastly different from that in the bustling hubbub of London, and working as a dressmaker could not have been more different from helping on the smallholding – while also trying to raise a family.

She found it very hard and she was, therefore, relieved when – not long after their third child was born – Jack decided to strike out anew. They sold the smallholding to his father and moved down to Cornwall, where Jack went into partnership with another small farmer. It was not the promised land. Within a year Peggy found herself back in Ambridge and pleased to be there, because at least she had all her husband's relatives to turn to for friendship and help. In Cornwall she had been very lonely.

Jack decided to give up farming and try his hand at something different. The war had unsettled him and he couldn't seem to apply himself to anything for very long. Peggy was worried about him and she was frankly horrified when he declared that he was going to take over the tenancy of the village pub. She changed her attitude, however, when they moved into the pub and found it was the centre of the village's social life. The noisy, busy bar was closer to what she had been used to in London.

Not long after the move, her husband started betting very heavily on the horses and she noticed he was beginning to drink quite heavily too. Within a year, things had got so bad that Borchester Brewery, who owned 'The Bull', threatened to revoke his licence and evict them. With a family of three to look after, she was panic-stricken and after long sessions with the company bosses she persuaded them to let them stay, but they made the condition that *she* became the licensee.

It took all her strength of character to make Jack accept the situation but – only because of the children – he finally agreed to swallow his pride. That was in 1953 and she held the licence for nearly twenty years before passing it on to the present licensee, Polly Perks.

In 1954, the strain told on Jack so much that he had to go into a mental hospital, and for four months Peggy was left to cope single-handed with the pub and family.

The next few years were far from easy, with Jack getting more and more unhappy about having to play second fiddle, as it were. At one stage he talked about going back into farming, and even went on a fruit-growing course. But he never quite got round to doing anything more positive and it was left to Peggy to keep things going.

During this time the ownership of 'The Bull' had changed hands, and in 1959, Stourhampton Breweries decided to sell it. They put it on the market at £5,300 and said they would only sell to a private landlord. They didn't want competition for their beer from another brewery! This meant that the new owner would almost certainly want to run it himself. It looked as if the Archers would be forced to go somewhere else because they clearly couldn't buy the place themselves. But it was another member of the Archer family who came to the rescue: Mrs Laura Archer, an aunt by marriage who had come to live in Ambridge from New Zealand a couple of years earlier when her husband died. He had left her very well off and she decided to invest in 'The Bull', putting up £4,000 towards the cost of buying the freehold.

With security for the family more or less guaranteed, Peggy was able to enjoy her role as the landlady of everyone's favourite country pub. And she was able to take a more active part in the general life of the village. But as things appeared to get better, her husband seemed to resent the situation and turned more and more to drink and gambling. This soon had its effect on the children, particularly the oldest girl, Jennifer. In 1967 she had an illegitimate baby, and it took all Peggy's strength of character to carry her through this period, with Jack wanting simply to throw Jennifer out of their home. When she refused even to consider it, his answer was again to hit the bottle hard.

He died in 1972 in a clinic in Scotland, while Peggy was up there visiting him. The shock was too much for her to carry on at 'The Bull' and she put in a temporary manager. When he ran away with the profits and half the liquor stock she was totally disillusioned and couldn't face going back. So she let it to Sid and Polly Perks, and took a job with local businessman, Mr Jack Woolley, helping to run his country club and other business affairs.

She moved into a flat at the club, and for a couple of years, things went well – until Mr Woolley suddenly proposed to her. She didn't want to remarry and she felt she couldn't go on working at the club under the circumstances, so she resigned and moved into a cottage rented from her new son-in-law, Ralph Bellamy. She also went back to work at 'The Bull', helping the Perks, but that didn't work out either. Sid and Polly obviously found having her around inhibited them too much and, being a sensitive woman, she left them to get on with it by themselves.

These days she is nearly content being a lady of leisure. But only *nearly*. She's already found another job, part-time secretary to the manager of her son-in-law's estate. She has always led a very active life and she doesn't really know how to cope with too much time on her hands. Working, she says, stops her interfering with her children's affairs! That's what you call an understanding mother.

Philip Archer

Following in father's footsteps is never easy. When your father has followed in his father's footsteps – and made a success of doing so – it becomes almost impossible. Nobody knows this better than Philip Archer, who, five years after becoming boss of Ambridge's Brookfield Farm, is still trying to get out from under his father's shadow.

Philip has been a very successful farmer in his own right for many years, and his father is the first to say so. But father is Dan Archer, and that is the problem. Dan

23

took over Brookfield when his father died and ran it for more than fifty years, building it into one of the most successful farms in the district, and consequently establishing himself as a popular and respected figure in Ambridge. His record takes an awful lot of beating. Not that there is any competition between father and son. It is simply that Philip is always seen as Dan's son and most of the time he really doesn't mind. But every now and then he would like to be known as his own man.

Another shadow that hung over Philip Archer's life for many years was the tragic death of his first wife, Grace. In September 1955 there was a terrible fire in her stables and she was trapped after rescuing the horses. She died in his arms in the ambulance on the way to hospital, less than six months after their wedding. His anguish was indescribable and it left him totally bewildered for a long time.

At the time he was farm manager for Grace's father, George Fairbrother, looking after the farming side of the business. And it was in farming that he sought release from the tensions created by his personal grief. He threw himself into his work with an almost frightening fury but it wasn't for two years that he found any sort of peace of mind.

At the village fête in 1957 he met a girl called Jill Patterson. He later bumped into her in Borchester, they dated, and by the end of the year they were married. They had twins, Kenton and Shula, the following year;

a son David a year later; and another daughter, Elizabeth, in 1967.

It was in the year the twins were born that Grace's father sold his interests in Ambridge to Charles Grenville. His ideas didn't really coincide with Philip's plans and Philip decided to strike out on his own. He bought a local farm and let the land to his father who was then establishing Ambridge Dairy Farmers Ltd and expanding the business. He let the farmhouse as holiday accommodation. A couple of years later, ADF Ltd acquired another farm and Philip was offered the tenancy. He took it on and immediately amalgamated with his father and another farmer to form Ambridge Farmers Ltd. At the same time he sold the other farm to Grenville. He built up his new farm – Hollowtree – and became highly successful in pig-breeding.

As his father moved towards retirement, Philip became the driving force in the company and eventually became chairman in 1970. Dan and Doris went into semi-retirement, living in Glebe Cottage, and there were few clouds around when Philip moved his family into Brookfield Farm. He'd had a long, long wait but it had all been worth it. His nephew Tony joined the board, having inherited his father's shares in the company, and his wife Jill became the company secretary. With the family very much in control, Philip eased off a little and found time to run the village scout troop and to organise a folk chorale for the 1973 festival.

The past eighteen months have not, however, been quite so bright. Tony left Brookfield to set up his own farm in partnership with Haydn Evans, although he did retain his shares. Philip then started an apprenticeship scheme and took on a young lad called Neil Carter. He'd never done any farmwork before and Philip found it very taxing trying to break him in. Then on top of that an outbreak of swine vesicular disease hit the farm and the whole herd had to be slaughtered. As the accounts showed, it had been a bad year, with the

25

company just about breaking even. But Philip Archer has been through darker times and he is optimistic about the future.

Shula Archer
Shula Archer, the eighteen-year-old local rider who took lessons from champion show-jumper Ann Moore, has now given up the idea of becoming a professional and instead plans to establish a riding scheme for disabled children. The twin daughter of Philip and Jill Archer, Shula has been riding since before she could even walk and has always said her ambition was to become a champion like Ann Moore.

Like her cousin Lilian, at whose stables she now works, Shula has always resisted her parents' attempts to steer her on a different career. They wanted her to become a vet, but her natural flair with horses – and Miss Moore's advice that she did have talent – eventually persuaded them to let her work at the stables.

Her acceptance that she just wasn't good enough to make the top grade as a show-jumper came last year, after she could get only two second places in a regional competition. Even though these would have given her entry to Hickstead, she decided not to go on. Now she is concentrating on studying horse-management. She already knows about the administrative side of running stables. After leaving Borchester Grammar School with A levels in English and Economics, she went to technical college and took a secretarial business course.

Now a very attractive blonde, Shula is much more popular in Ambridge than she was as a child. She was very precocious and was always creating some disturbance or another in the rural calm. When her father gave her a cine camera as a fourteenth-birthday present, she plagued the life out of everyone by making what she described as a documentary of the village. Then she became a vegetarian and staged a protest at her father's pig-breeding unit. There were other incidents and she always seemed to be rowing with her twin, Kenton. But she was genuinely upset when he left home to join the Merchant Navy. She felt guilty that she may have been responsible for him wanting to leave home!

If she is successful in launching her proposed scheme, she will be giving lessons to handicapped children from all over the county. 'It's a very exciting project because I'll be sharing some of the tremendous pleasures I've had from riding with children who might not otherwise ever get near a horse,' she says. The whole village is behind her and if enthusiasm is a guide, the scheme is certain to be a winner.

Tony Archer
When Tony Archer's father died and left him a considerable shareholding in Ambridge Farmers Ltd, he could have joined his grandfather and uncle in the highly successful company. Instead, he decided to retain his independence and went into partnership with Haydn Evans at Willow Farm, a new venture with an uncertain future. No one, however, was unduly surprised because Tony was almost notorious for his independent streak. Being brought up with two older sisters, he says he had to be independent or he would have been smothered by their attentions. Certainly at school he was seen as a loner who never wanted to join in team games, but who excelled in areas like long-distance running.

When he left school, he declined offers to work at Brookfield Farm with his grandfather and took a job on the Bellamy Estate. He did very well there, and Mr Bellamy persuaded him to go for training to the Walford Farm Institute. He enjoyed his year at Walford, particularly because much of the course was practical work and gave him full scope for using his own initiative. He got excellent reports and the lecturers all said he had a bright future in farming.

All these complimentary remarks rather went to his head, and back in Ambridge he started expounding his new-found theories, convinced that only he knew what was best for the estate. Mr Bellamy took it all very well and even encouraged him to go on to a farm management course at Borchester Technical College. His family, however, didn't react quite so generously, especially his father who didn't want him to go into farming anyway. Jack Archer had never been a successful farmer and, in fact, had even given up his smallholding to become a publican. He was the sort of man who didn't like the thought of his son making a go of something at which he'd failed. He tried to press Tony into a career at 'The Bull'.

The constant rows upset Tony. At one stage he considered emigrating but decided against it and tried to settle down working for Ralph Bellamy. He took on the secretaryship of the local branch of the National Union of Agricultural Workers, went on various specialist courses and generally tried to apply himself to becoming a good farmer. But then other distractions started coming into play, and he had a whole string of girl friends who kept his mind off his job. In the end, after one or two disasters on the estate, it all proved too much for Bellamy and – despite the fact that they had since become in-laws when Bellamy married Tony's sister, Lilian – he was fired.

The blow to his pride was severe and his immediate reaction was to get well away from Ambridge. So he went to France for a long holiday and, when he came back, he'd swallowed his pride sufficiently to go to work for the family company. This actually took a lot of courage, because it was only months before, after inheriting his father's shares, that he'd refused to join his grandfather, Dan Archer. At Brookfield he got on quite well with his grandfather, but his Uncle Phil didn't take so kindly to his whiz-kid ways, and they had regular arguments.

Frustrated at not being in charge, Tony sought another outlet for his management skills – he became player-manager of the village football team! He actually did quite well at that and the team had a run of very good results but, of course, it wasn't enough and he soon became bored with life. In the end he left Brookfield, retaining his shares, and went into partnership with Haydn Evans at Willow Farm.

At Willow Farm he began building up a dairy herd and soon began to show signs of being successful. He also became engaged to the girl who came in to do the paper work for Mr Evans, Mary Weston. That relationship, however, ended as quickly as it started and, while she was on holiday in Majorca, she wrote suggesting they call off the proposed wedding. With his pride again shattered, Tony was desolate. Not, however, for very long. His natural ebullience saw him through what he described as the 'dark days', and he was soon dating several other girls, enjoying driving around the countryside in his open-topped sports car with one or other of them always beside him.

Then he met Pat Lewis. Pat was a very attractive Welsh girl, niece of his partner Haydn Evans, and when she came for a few days' visit he fell for her. He sold the sports car and bought a much more useful van. He redoubled his efforts in building up the farm, proposed to Pat, and was delighted when she accepted.

They were married just before Christmas last year and they are now expecting their first child. Both are

29

hoping that it will be a boy who will one day carry on the Archer tradition of farming in Ambridge.

Gordon Armstrong

Young Gordon Armstrong is a classic example of the townsman who got fed up with the hurly-burly of urban life and a sought escape in the countryside. He used to live in Newcastle, where he wrote nature notes for the local paper. This gave him such a strong interest in country life that he decided to take a full-time course in gamekeeping. After that he applied for, and got, the job as assistant keeper to Tom Forrest, and has been in Ambridge since the spring of 1971.

He still writes nature notes but his other interests are less peaceful – judo and playing football for Ambridge Wanderers. It was he who built up the wildfowl when Jack Woolley developed his country park, and when Tom Forrest was promoted to become sporting manager, he was very disappointed not to get Tom's job. He found it difficult to accept that his lack of experience was a considerable drawback. He did try to find another job but was unsuccessful, and decided to stay on in Ambridge, where he has made many friends.

George Barford

George Barford came to Ambridge in 1973 as gamekeeper to Jack Woolley. He replaced Tom Forrest but worked under him in his new capacity as sporting manager. You couldn't find two men so different from each other. Tom Forrest, happy and friendly; George Barford, morose and introvert. He is very much a loner and at first he was something of a mystery figure in the village. It was some time before anyone knew more than that he had worked on Lord Netherbourne's estate at the other end of the county. Then Colin Drury, the village policeman, found that Barford too had once been in the force. His anti-social habits precluded anyone from making friends and it soon became clear he had drink problems. Just how serious these were no one knew until he tried to commit suicide, and it was then discovered he had been an alcoholic.

The new vicar, who had been with the Samaritans in Birmingham and was now with the Borchester group, was able to help. So too was Nora McAuley who worked at 'The Bull'. Barford tried to resist all help, especially Nora's because she was obviously getting too fond of him and, although separated, he was still married and his wife, a Roman Catholic, would not divorce him. But she was not to be put off and eventually she moved into Lodge Cottage to live with him. He didn't like the situation and Nora decided to leave – without telling him she was by now pregnant.

In fact finding this out was perhaps the best thing that could have happened, because it changed him completely. When she had a miscarriage he was kindness itself, and they are now very happy together. He has come out of his shell a bit, and even goes to local football matches and shouts for Ambridge Wanderers!

James Barnett
James Barnett is the latest Birmingham businessman to move out into the country. When the Bellamy estate was broken up last year, he bought part of it and created his own Blossom Hill Estate. But whereas others, such as Jack Woolley, have integrated into and adapted to country life, Mr Barnett doesn't seem to want to do that. Instead of employing local farmworkers, he has brought in contract-workers to run the estate. The NFU and the farm-workers' union are watching the situation with keen interest.

James Bellamy
Although not yet three, little James Bellamy is destined to become one of the biggest landowners in Ambridge. Although his father, the former squire, has sold off most of his land, he has retained a large acreage which he

hopes to transfer one day to James. Just when that will happen depends very largely on the taxman. Under the present tax regulations, such a transfer would be prohibitive.

Lilian Bellamy

Anyone who imagines the life of a modern country squire to be one of gracious comfort should talk to Mrs Bellamy. She would, no doubt, quickly disillusion them for she has seen the effect on her husband's health of the uphill struggle to hold together a large estate in today's economic climate. She is certain that it was only his premature retirement and their extensive world cruise that has saved his health from being permanently damaged.

Before she married Ralph Bellamy, Squire of Ambridge, in 1971, Lilian had no idea just how tough a life he had to lead. Her background – she was the daughter of Mr and Mrs Jack Archer, who ran the local pub – was very different, and the way of life of the landed gentry was beyond her ken. She was brought up like most of the village girls, going to the local infants school and eventually on to Borchester Grammar. She did quite well there and, when she got several GCE O levels, her parents thought she might become a vet. But it was her hobby rather than her academic success that actually shaped her career – she was simply mad on horses. She started riding when she was about ten and got her first pony, which she called 'Pensioner', when she was fourteen. From then on it was pretty pointless for her parents to imagine her doing anything not involving horses. The vet idea was a compromise.

Lilian, however, wasn't interested in compromise. Vets only look after horses when they are sick, and she wanted to look after them all the time. Her parents conceded and she was sent to a riding academy at Felpersham. She found the discipline there somewhat severe and left after a few months, but later realised it was for her benefit and she went back and completed the course, showing considerable determination for such a young girl.

She was still not quite eighteen when she went into partnership with another local girl, Valerie Woolley, to run riding stables at Grey Gables. A couple of years later she set up on her own after taking her instructor's certificate and buying three horses and four ponies.

Around this time, her sister, Jennifer, created a local scandal by having an illegitimate child. Lilian was terribly shocked by the incident but very quickly suppressed her own feelings to stand by her older sister when so many others were turning against her. That was another sign of the strength of her character and Jennifer was very grateful for her support.

Lilian herself needed emotional support not many years later. She met a young Canadian pilot called Lester Nicholson. He was invalided out of the Canadian air force because of ear trouble and they were married in this country in May 1969. Less than ten months later he died in a Canadian hospital where he had gone for treatment. It was her turn to need her family's support. Being a widow at twenty-one was not easy, even in a village community where people tend to rally round in such circumstances. To help herself get over the shock, Lilian again threw herself into her work at the stables and being with her beloved horses proved to be the therapy she needed.

Later that year, she met Ralph Bellamy at a local function and they naturally talked about the problems of not having a partner on such occasions. He then asked if she would consider acting as hostess for him at a dinner party he was giving. She agreed and their friendship blossomed. She took on his horse, Red Knight, for exercising, and then rode him to victory in the point-to-point Ladies' Race.

Eighteen months after Lester's death, Lilian married the Squire and the wedding was the social occasion of the year in Ambridge. Lilian's only sadness was that her father could not be present. He was seriously ill in the Scottish hospital where he later died.

After honeymooning at the Lido in Venice, Lilian and Ralph moved into the newly-decorated Dower House and Lilian started planning the extension of her riding-school activities. At the same time Ralph bought more land – the estate of the late Brigadier Winstanley – and she began to see just how much work was involved in running the estate. Her younger brother, Tony, didn't help matters. He worked for Ralph but he had been acting with a frightening lack of responsibility and was sacked. This added to the already heavy burden on the Squire. When their son, James, was born, he seemed to work even harder, and eventually Lilian had to call in the doctor to persuade Ralph to take things more easily. Finally he succumbed to the pressure and surprised everyone by deciding to sell up most of his land. Now he, Lilian and young James are enjoying their world trip, although they look forward to returning to Ambridge in the not-too-distant future.

Ralph Bellamy

When Ralph Bellamy inherited his father's country estate, he gave up the high life in London and moved to Ambridge with every intention of becoming the village squire. Sadly he devoted so much time and energy towards realising his ambition that it affected his health and forced him into premature retirement only three short years after taking on the squire's role.

It was in 1964 that he came back to Ambridge and he

immediately set about reorganising the estate's affairs. He sold off various parts of the business and, in partnership with Jack Woolley, bought up the Grenville estate. They worked out a comprehensive scheme to redevelop but ran into local opposition and the idea was rejected by the planning authorities. Undeterred, Ralph simply turned back to farming – but on a bigger scale – and joining a co-operative scheme with the then squire, Brigadier Winstanley. He also started diversifying by buying a small engineering firm and then a garage at Penny Hassett.

By 1970 he had transformed the running of the estate into a highly-efficient business operation epitomised, on the land by the use of the very latest equipment including the driverless tractor, and in the office by the use of computer accountancy. He had increased the profitability four-fold. His driving ambition made him unpopular with many of the local people, whose natural conservatism militated against so much change so quickly, but he let nothing stand in his way.

When Brigadier Winstanley died, he decided without hesitation to buy up all the land that became available, and with his newly-enlarged estate he also became the undisputed squire of Ambridge. It had taken him three years less than the ten-year target he had privately set himself.

His new position, however, made him more conscious of the need for a wife to grace his social occasions. As he had become more and more important in the farming world, he had taken to asking various ladies to act as hostess when he gave dinner parties, although he was much too busy to become more than acquainted with the women in his circle. One of these was Mrs Lilian Nicholson, a young Ambridge widow, and grand-daughter of Dan and Doris Archer. She had also been looking after his horse at her stables and they had been riding together once or twice. She wasn't quite the sort of girl he would have chosen if he had been still living in London, but she did fit in well to the Ambridge scene and he proposed to her. After a good deal of heart-searching – because of her feelings for her dead husband and the age difference between her and Ralph – she finally accepted and they were married in September 1971. The wedding was the social occasion of the year in the county.

His new responsibilities did slow him down a little, but not for very long and he was soon expanding his business interests even further by buying and reopening the village garage. He also became more and more involved with village activities and in 1973 he took over as chairman of the soccer team, Ambridge Wanderers. But the strain soon began to tell and he became more and more tetchy with everyone and this was only helped slightly by the birth of his son and heir, James.

Matters seemed to come to a head when there was a row between Ralph and the agricultural workers' union over tied cottages. His doctor ordered him to rest and then later suggested that he should give up working altogether. For a man who had been so active and who had so much driving ambition, the idea of quietly stepping down was anathema and he tried to bluster his way through. But then he realised that it wasn't only his own interests he had to protect, but those of Lilian and their son. Just as he had done on so many previous occasions, he made up his mind and swiftly opted out, acting on his decision with astonishing speed. He sold most of his land, keeping only 1000 acres as a future

36

investment for James, and left Ambridge for an in-
definite trip to various parts of the world.

He has so far spent a lot of time cruising in warmer
climes and, as a former Navy commander, he has
relaxed and enjoyed the sea air. According to Lilian in
her letters home, he has never looked fitter.

Rose Blossom

Mrs Rose Blossom, housekeeper to two squires of
Ambridge, is nearing seventy, but still has no intention
of retiring. She now works for Arnold Lucas, the man
who rented the Dower House after the Bellamys left
and who now lives there almost as a recluse. She is his
only regular contact with the villages.

Mrs Blossom came to Ambridge with Brigadier
Winstanley in 1969. When he died, she decided to stay
on and keep house for Ralph and Lilian Bellamy,
although she refused to live in and took a bungalow of
her own.

Harry Booker

Harry Booker, Ambridge's postman, wears his uniform
with that extra swagger that only old soldiers have.
Married to a local farmer's daughter, he came to the
village in 1973 straight from ten years in the army. He
had been a sergeant and, despite pressure from his
father-in-law, Ken Pound, he wouldn't take a job in
farming. He preferred to join a Borchester transport
company as a driver, and for a while he drove the
mini-bus which served Ambridge. When that service
was scrapped because it wasn't paying, he drove the
school bus and doubled as the company's taxi-driver.
He switched to the Post Office when they launched the
new Post-bus scheme.

Harry's army training has also proved useful in his
spare-time activities. He runs the cricket team and
keeps the football team fit.

Heather Brammidge

If some of Ambridge's women are walking taller these days, you can thank Mrs Heather Brammidge. She is the young schoolteacher from nearby Lyttleton who has been giving them keep-fit exercises at the Women's Institute. Mrs Brammidge, a former international gymnast, has aimed the exercises at improving posture as well as general fitness.

Joan Burton

Mrs Joan Burton is probably Ambridge's most determined resident. When she was a teenager and her family left to go back to Scotland, she ran away and came back to the village on her own.

At that time her uncle ran the bakery and she thought he would let her stay with him, but he was worried about her and sent her back to her parents. Even that didn't deter her, for when she was old enough she came back again and got a job with a market gardener. She later studied at Studely Agricultural College and then worked for the then estate-owner, Charles Grenville. She gave that up to become a full-time farmer's wife in 1964.

Nigel Burton

When Nigel Burton came to Ambridge in 1961, he didn't really intend staying. He was a farmhand with something of an itinerant nature and he was quite honest with Dan Archer, who gave him a job at Brookfield Farm, that he would probably only stay for a couple of years at the very most. He actually stayed for more than three years and when he left it was to run his own farm as a tenant on the local estate – with a local girl, Joan Hood, as his wife. They have a daughter, Juliet, who is now eleven and goes to school in Borchester.

Neil Carter

When Neil Carter arrived in Ambridge in 1973, he was a skinny sixteen-year-old townie and Brookfield Farms' first apprentice. Today he is a broad-shouldered young man with a promising career in farming ahead of him.

Although born in Oxfordshire, Neil came to the village from Birmingham where he had spent most of his life. He joined Ambridge Farmers Ltd under a 'new-entrant' scheme run by the Agricultural Training Committee. This meant that, while working on the farm most of the time, he was also given time off to go to day-release classes at Borchester Technical College and for other studies.

He didn't take to his new life very well in the early days. The work was hard and the hours long and he didn't like the 'mothering' he got from his landlady. His own background was that of an unstable home and he just couldn't understand that she was simply concerned for his well-being. He saw it as interfering. Gradually, as he began to understand why the various jobs on the farm had to be done in certain ways at certain times, he became a very useful member of the small work force. It also helped him settle into village life. He was found to have a good singing voice and was pressed into joining the Ambridge Folk Chorale. Then he started making friends with the other teenagers in the district.

He got into trouble with the police at one stage, not long after taking a part-time job at a Borchester pub. He was at a party when there was a drug raid, and he was charged and put on probation, and made the subject of a community service order. His boss, Philip Archer, was very disappointed when Neil failed his proficiency test on safety grounds and then very angry when he discovered that he had also been skipping some of his day-release classes. However, Philip put down most of these incidents to Neil's background and the general problems of growing up. For his part, Neil seemed to pull himself together and is now doing very well at Brookfield.

Susan Cattermole
Raising a family of seven growing children on a labourer's wages of about £35 a week is not easy, and when Mrs Susan Cattermole resorted to stealing food from the village shop, few people were surprised.

Mrs Cattermole, who lives in the council houses, aroused more sympathy than anger – even from the shop assistant who was originally suspected of pilfering. Her problems are increased even further by the drinking habits of her husband. While she struggles to make ends meet, he can be found every night in the 'Cat and Fiddle' pub.

Jack Woolley, proprietor of the shop, decided against prosecution and Mrs Cattermole was very grateful. It even had some effect on her husband. He now misses the odd night out at the pub!

Eileen Dickson
Quietly-spoken Mrs Eileen Dickson, matron and house-keeper at the Field Centre, is a former army nurse who was injured serving in France during the war. Her husband was killed in 1943, trying to escape from a German prisoner-of-war camp, and she came to the Centre in 1974 from a teaching post in a London hospital.

Barbara Drury
Mrs Barbara Drury, wife of the village bobby, is a big-city girl who can't quite get used to living in the country even though she has been in Ambridge for nearly ten years.

She was brought up in a large family in Leeds, and found the transition from a big council house in the bustling city to the little police cottage in Ambridge very difficult. The result was to increase her shyness and it wasn't until last year that she played any part in the village social life. Then it was to make her début in the ladies' soccer team! She has now also joined the Women's Institute.

Colin Drury
Colin Drury was Ambridge's last village bobby in the old tradition of bicycle clips and big boots. He is also the first in the new style of Panda cars, two-way radios and so on. He joined the police force in Borchester and came to Ambridge in 1967, as soon as his probationary period was up. When the county force was reorganised in 1971, he was withdrawn and went back to head-quarters, but within a year he returned to live in the village. He was given a Panda car and a larger patch – from Penny Hassett right across to Hollerton.

Constable Drury is very much a product of his age. He has all the basic qualities of the old bobby – firm but friendly, a tower of strength in any emergency. But he also has the young policeman's tendency to be punctilious, a stickler for adhering to the absolute letter of the law. This means that he doesn't always find his job very easy in a tightly-knit community like Ambridge.

Joe Dunnington
When the village smithy stood under the spreading chestnut tree, the large and brawny arms belonged to Joe Dunnington, the third generation of his family to run the forge. Today the smithy has disappeared but Joe, now nearly sixty-five, still plies his ancient trade – from the back of an old van. He is now a travelling blacksmith and serves almost half the county.

James Elland
Ambridge doesn't run to its own bank, but it does have a bank manager. When James Elland was appointed to the bank in Hollerton in 1972, he bought a house in Ambridge, and is now a popular figure around the village. He is married and has two children.

Madge Elliott

Mrs Madge Elliott, widow of an army major, was one of the first tenants to move into Hollowtree Flats when they were completed in 1971. She is a shy, introvert lady who keeps very much to herself, and all the villagers seem to know about her is that she likes gin! They deduce this from the regular deliveries made by a Borchester wine merchant.

Haydn Evans

Few people can have settled in and become part of the community more easily and readily than Welshman Haydn Evans. It's less than three years since he came to Ambridge from his native Carmarthenshire, but already he is deeply involved in village affairs and is clerk to the Parish Council.

Haydn, a warm, friendly man, brought his lilting accent to Ambridge when his wife died back home in Wales. He bought some land near Lakey Hill and, with his son Gwyn, started a new venture – Willow Farm. It was perhaps the tremendous courage he showed in starting a new farm that first endeared him to the villagers. Certainly when he ran into difficulties, there was no shortage of offers of help and he accepted it gratefully.

In the first year his son became ill and then quietly eloped with one of the village girls, leaving Haydn trying to cope single-handed. The next year, he had more trouble. First some of his cows were stolen and then the silage effluent from his farm got into the stream running into the country park, killing thousands of fish.

Others might have given up at this stage, but Haydn simply decided to take in a partner, and he was joined by young Tony Archer. However, when he slipped a disc less than a year later, he did accept defeat and gave up farming completely. Instead, he bought the local garage and is now literally at the centre of village life.

Pru Forrest

As the wife of the local gamekeeper, you might expect Mrs Pru Forrest to have a larder well stocked with rabbits, game birds and the like, but she hasn't. She doesn't like that sort of meat and hates the business of skinning, plucking and gutting so much that she has long since dissuaded Tom from bringing them home.

She would also contend that she is, in any case, much too busy to spare all the time needed for the preparation. Since her older boy, Johnnie, left home, she has started working again. She helps out at Brookfield Farm, and for a time she also went back to her old job as barmaid at 'The Bull'. But that came to an end because the pub ran into economic difficulties. She was very annoyed at getting the sack and created quite a fuss at the time. As always, Tom jollied her back into a good humour and relationships between her and Sid Perks are now restored to normality.

Tom Forrest

No one knows the countryside around Ambridge better than Tom Forrest. For forty years, he has walked the land as gamekeeper to the local squires and landowners, keeping a watchful eye on the wildlife and discouraging all but the most determined poachers.

Today he has the fancy title of sporting manager – bestowed on him by his latest boss, Jack Woolley – but he is still very much the gamekeeper – and always will be. For him it isn't a job but his whole way of life, helping, as he puts it, to keep the natural life as natural as possible.

His first walk around the squire's estate was at the knee of his elder brother Ted, when he was just eight and Ted was one of the junior keepers. Trying to keep pace with Ted's easy gait as they tramped through the woods and across the meadows, Tom decided then that he would become a gamekeeper. Even his brother's tragic death in a shooting accident a year or so later didn't dissuade him.

The only time he has ever regretted that early decision was in 1957, when he too was involved in a shooting accident – but an accident that led to him being charged with murder. The accident happened one night when Tom was keeping watch for poachers who had been stealing a lot of birds from the estate. He caught one of the men, there was a fight, and in the struggle Tom's gun went off, killing the man. It might all have ended there, written off as a tragic accident, if the dead man hadn't been Ned Larkin's brother Bob. For some time before the incident he had been pestering Tom's girlfriend, Pru, barmaid at the local pub, and he and Tom had rowed about it. Someone had also heard Tom threaten to 'bash Bob Larkin's face for him'.

That, and the fact that the police didn't find any evidence of a struggle at the scene, made things look black for Tom although the charge was reduced from murder to manslaughter before it went to court. It was only after some of his friends had traced Bob Larkin's movements earlier in the evening, and discovered he had been in a pub and talking about going poaching that Tom was finally acquitted – much to his relief and the delight of the whole village, which welcomed him home with a silver band and a great reception.

The episode brought him and Pru even closer together and they married the next year. When they later discovered that they couldn't have children of their own, they decided to foster and they had first Johnnie Martin and later Peter Stevens. Despite some initial problems, both boys stayed to make Ambridge their home.

Peter, the younger of the two boys, did cause Tom particular embarrassment during his adolescence, when he got caught poaching with a gang of schoolboys. Luckily for Peter, who was not quite fifteen at the time, Pru saw the funny side of the situation and she was able to make Tom see it that way too.

A few years later, it was Tom's turn to see the funny side of an otherwise tricky situation. Pru had gone to work at 'The Bull' part-time and, when Sid and Polly Perks ran into money problems and were forced to cut back on staff, she was the first to be laid off. She took it very badly and forbade Tom to go into 'The Bull'. Tom, a loyal man, adhered to the letter of her demands. He didn't go into 'The Bull' – but he did hang around outside while the other regulars brought him free drinks out of sympathy. As a result, he ended up tiddly – to the consternation of Pru. But she did lift the ban.

During his long years working for the landed gentry, Tom has needed his sense of humour on more than one occasion. His first employer was Squire Lawson-Hope, and they got on so well together that, when he left, he gave Tom a small life-pension and fixed a job for him with his successor, Mr Fairbrother. But Tom didn't always see eye-to-eye with his later bosses and often had to bite his tongue when he worked for Charles Grenville and again when Ralph Bellamy bought the estate.

It was when Jack Woolley opened the Ambridge Country Park and took over the shoot that Tom first worked for him and became his sporting manager. It is perhaps a surprising partnership: Mr Woolley, a sharp-tongued businessman from Birmingham, and Tom Forrest, a gently-spoken countryman. But it works because the two respect each other and perhaps recognise qualities in the other that are missing from their own make-up.

Whatever it is, Tom is held in the highest regard by Mr Woolley, just as he has been by most of his employers over the past forty years.

Nelson Gabriel

Seeing the two together, you would never guess that Walter and Nelson Gabriel are father and son – except perhaps for the glint of pride in the old man's eye. They are as different as it is possible to be. Walter is a gnarled old countryman with an accent to match, and a dress-sense that would give a scarecrow encouragement. Nelson is a smooth-tongued, city type whose tailor clearly graduated from Saville Row.

Nelson left Ambridge to do his National Service in the RAF and liked the life so much that he signed on as a regular, serving in exotic spots around the world. His flight-sergeant's pay and the tax-free overseas allowances gave him plenty of opportunity to develop a taste for the high life. When he left, however, he could no longer afford to live in style and he was soon up to his eyes in debt and had to turn to his father for help. Walter cleared his debts and later helped him set up in a small engineering business in Borchester.

He ran this successfully for several years but sold out in 1966 and used the profits to buy a partnership in a casino and two betting shops. This was the beginning of a very shady part of his life in which he was reported missing but then turned up in Ambridge and was in some way involved in a mail-van robbery. He disappeared again immediately afterwards and it took Interpol several months before they caught up with him on the continent and brought him back to England for trial. To Walter's relief and everyone else's astonishment he was acquitted, and then moved to Surrey to get away from the bad publicity.

The shock of the trial did, however, put him back on the straight and narrow. At least if some of his recent business operations have seemed dubious, they are certainly on the right side of the law, and his acquisition of Hollowtree Farmhouse and its conversion into flats was a perfectly normal business transaction.

Walter Gabriel

Walter Gabriel has been one of Ambridge's 'characters' for more years than he would ever admit. He is as coy as any woman when it comes to being specific about his age although he doesn't deny being over twenty-one. As he can – and all too often does – recall the vivid events leading up to the First World War, it is safe to assume that he is quite a bit over twenty-one!

Walter has always lived in the village and, like most of his contemporaries, he left the local school with the sketchiest of educations to go straight on to the land as a farmworker. But he never liked the rigid discipline of farmlife, regulated as it is by the needs of the animals, and even when he had his own farm he wasn't devoted enough to be successful.

In fact, when his wife died and his only son Nelson went into the RAF in the early fifties, he simply let the farm run down, and as a result was always in trouble with his landlord, the local squire, until he eventually gave up in 1957.

Since then, shed of all his responsibilities, Walter has played havoc in Ambridge with a whole string of entrepreneurial ventures that have left the villagers variously bemused, bothered and bewildered. Not that

47

he had done badly in that respect in earlier years. For example, when he was a member of Dad's Army – the Home Guard – during the last war, his most significant strike against the foe was when he blew up one of his neighbour's scarecrows by mistake!

The villagers did once see some hope of a peaceful life – when Walter heard that an old uncle had died in Australia, leaving him a partnership in a gold mine *and* a sheep-farm. Before you could skin a kangaroo, Walter's plans had him Down Under to help rake in the money and his neighbours were as happy for him as they were for themselves!

Sadly, everyone's joy was short-lived. The inheritance was real enough and Walter was the new partner in the Yellow Lodestone and Merino Wool Trading Company of Woolagong. The drawback was simply that the company had no assets, not even enough to pay Walter's bus fare to Borchester. He had to settle for a dream of what might have been – and the long-suffering residents of Ambridge had to go on suffering.

His first venture after giving up the farm was to buy a mini-bus and set himself up as the village carrier. All went well until he tried to combine the carriage of passengers with the transportation of livestock. Neither side were particularly happy with the arrangement.

In the Christmas of that year, there was a tiny incident that showed Walter up as the kindly old man that he is, instead of the old rogue that he pretends to be. He won the giant food hamper in the annual village raffle and was planning to ask his favourite lady-friend, Mrs Perkins, to share it with him, when he found a little girl crying on the green outside the village hall. She had saved up and bought two tickets in the raffle, convinced that she would win the hamper for her family, who wouldn't otherwise have had any Christmas dinner. Without a moment's hesitation, Walter explained that there had been a mix-up over the draw and her ticket had won, and he, in fact, was on his way to deliver the hamper to her house.

Charity, of course, begins at home and when his son, Nelson, got himself into debt, Walter was quick to help him out of his trouble and later helped set him up in an engineering business in Borchester. But then, as far as Walter is concerned, his son can do no wrong and even when he got into serious trouble with the police, Walter stood by him throughout.

Nelson's tangle with the law was certainly a blow to Walter's pride although he did try to hide it. He was even less successful at hiding it when Mrs Perkins suddenly decided she was to remarry and Walter was not to be the lucky man. He was her namesake, Arthur Perkins, a stonemason.

Walter's reaction was to go into a different sort of partnership – with Ned Larkin in a pig-breeding venture. That bowled along quite nicely until he upset one of his neighbours, Mrs Turvey, over a deal to supply her with some pigs. It says a lot for Walter's guile that the dispute was resolved amicably, and only a few months later Mrs Turvey joined him and Bill Sawyer in opening a pet-shop in Borchester. Working with the animals in the shop set him off thinking on a grander scale than ever before, and he bought two elephants! He called the elephants Rosie and Tiny Tim, added two seals – Mutt and Jeff – and declared himself to be in the fairground sideshow business.

If his money-making exploits have shaken Ambridge metaphorically, some of his hobbies have shaken it literally. He used to disturb the peace by making ear-shattering noises on a trombone and, more recently, when indulging in the seemingly-harmless pastime of making home-brewed beer, he caused an explosion that was heard all over the village!

It seems that nothing is sacred or safe in Walter's hands and the villagers can only wait and wonder what on earth he's going to get up to next.

Richard Grenville

Richard Grenville is the fourteen-year-old son of Mrs Carol Tregorran and Charles Grenville, her first husband who died after a car crash. He is at boarding school where he is only now beginning to settle down again after a difficult time last year. When his step-father was away in America for several months, Richard was very unhappy and his way of attracting attention was to steal things from his schoolmates and make sure he was caught. He is now studying for his O levels and hopes to go on to take A levels and then go to University.

Joe Grundy

Tenant-farmer Joe Grundy sees himself as Ambridge's Mr Showbiz – though the other villagers tend to see him in an entirely different light. He upset locals by letting his field be used for a noisy autocross meeting and then for an even noisier pop festival. Mr Grundy's impresario pretensions would perhaps go down better if he ran the farm with the same enthusiasm as he does his money-making ploys. A widower, he and his two sons have made little effort to farm the land on the local estate and a few years back he was served with notice to quit because it had deteriorated so much. He only got out of it by making a special effort to tidy the place up, and since then he seems to have tried hard to keep one step ahead of the landlord.

He has a chip on his shoulder and reacts by causing as much trouble around the village as possible. When he was given notice to quit, his response was to threaten to shoot any deer that might stray on to his land from the nearby country park. Like the barrack-room lawyer that he is, he often uses the law to terrorise his victims. For example, when gamekeeper Tom Forrest said he was involved with selling venison to a Borchester hotel, he tried to sue him for slander.

Despite all this, he did get the sympathy of villagers when he went into hospital suffering from Farmer's Lung, and when he came out they went as far as co-opting him to fill a vacancy on the Parish Council after he had failed to win a seat at the annual elections. He repaid their kindness by creating a caravan site without permission, ignoring their protests about the autocross, and pressing on with the pop festival. It's hardly surprising that relations between him and the other villagers are all too often close to breaking point.

Alice Hart
The domestic bursar at Ambridge's Field Centre, Mrs Alice Hart is used to dealing with problems on a grand scale. She used to be on the staff at Buckingham Palace. She was a junior housekeeper in the Royal household and her duties included looking after the private quarters of the royal equerries. She lived in at the Palace and was directly responsible for a staff of eleven. Now twenty-six, she left to marry a Borchester bank official and lives in a small cottage at Penny Hassett.

Charles Harvey
When Charles Harvey bought part of a local estate and brought his family to live in Bull Farm, he was killing two birds with one stone: making a very shrewd investment and cutting down on his travelling time. Mr Harvey is an accountant with a very busy practice in London, but he has to travel all over England on clients' business. When he saw Bull Farm advertised, he realised it was ideally situated in the very centre of England, and it happened to be a bargain as well.

Since he and his family moved in last year, he hasn't had much time to enjoy the country life, but he is hoping to cut back on his business activities over the next few years and intends to play a part in the community life of Ambridge.

Jean Harvey

While her husband may not have yet settled into Ambridge, Mrs Jean Harvey certainly has. She is a born organiser and is already involved with various village activities, including the church appeal fund. Unfortunately, her big-city ways don't always endear her to the locals, and she has trodden on several people's corns in her efforts to be helpful.

Susan Harvey

Already a member of the village ladies' football team, twenty-three-year-old Susan Harvey could give her mother lessons in integration. She is very popular with everyone, probably because she so obviously enjoys living in the country. It gives her plenty of opportunity for riding her horse, Kelly.

Irene Jenkins

When anyone in Ambridge is sick they can always be sure of a friendly word from Mrs Irene Jenkins, receptionist at the village doctor's surgery for more than twenty years. Mrs Jenkins, a widow, not only arranges all the doctor's appointments and visits, but makes 'visits' of her own delivering prescriptions to people who find it difficult to get to the surgery. Her little bit of do-gooding, as she calls it, began one day when the doctor's car broke down and she went on her bicycle to deliver some pills to one of the outlying farms. She got so much pleasure out of the patient's relief that she quickly made it a feature of her 'service'. When Dr McLaren arrived in 1959, he was delighted to encourage its continuance.

Christine Johnson

When Mrs Christine Johnson took over the local stables and riding-school last year, she was turning the clock back nearly fifteen years. She now looks after the business for her niece, Mrs Lilian Bellamy, while the

latter is away from Ambridge on a world tour with her husband, but fifteen years ago she was the proprietor of her own stables. She gave up the business shortly after her marriage to Paul Johnson.

Christine, only daughter of Dan and Doris Archer, learned to ride almost as soon as she could walk and it was always her ambition to be boss of her own stables. She realised that ambition by the time she was twenty-one by going into partnership with a girl friend, Grace Fairbrother. Grace married Christine's brother Philip, but died tragically less than six months later in a fire at the stables.

Like everyone else in the village Christine was shattered by the tragedy, but she was helped by the need to go on looking after the horses and the continuing activity saw her through. She married a year later but soon found the business and her show-jumping activities didn't leave much time for a home life. Under pressure from Paul, she sold the stables and then, after a bad fall in which she broke two ribs and her collarbone, she also gave up competition jumping.

It wasn't until 1968, when she looked after the riding-school for a month while Lilian was on holiday, that she started riding again, and then only for pleasure. Instead she concentrated on bringing up their adopted son, Peter, and being part of village life, joining the Women's Institute, and so on.

Fred Johnson

Fred Johnson has done more than most to keep Ambridge alive: he is the proprietor of Borchester's biggest transport company. He runs the only taxi service in the district and provides the coaches to take the village children to school.

Paul Johnson

When Paul Johnson owned Ambridge's one and only garage and served the petrol, he never thought that one day he'd be at the other end of the business – drilling for oil in the North Sea. He doesn't actually do any drilling himself, but the company he now works for makes equipment for the oil rigs and he goes out to them regularly.

Although his main office is in London, Paul still lives in Ambridge with his wife Christine and their adopted son, Peter. He is away from home a lot, but the couple have got used to his travels by now. At one time he worked as a helicopter pilot and more recently he owned a small manufacturing business and both took him all over Europe.

Clarrie Larkin

At nineteen, Clarrie Larkin can only be described as a buxom lass who likes her food. The elder daughter of Lizzie and Jethro Larkin, she has had a weight problem most of her life, and working in the kitchen of 'The Bull' doesn't really help. It gives her the chance of eating almost non-stop. But as is so often the case with fat people, Clarrie has a delightfully cheerful personality and doesn't mind her shape in the least.

Jethro Larkin

Jethro Larkin's life on the land shows in every line of his tanned and healthy face. Although he is well into his forties, he is still fit enough to play football regularly for Ambridge Wanderers, and he can still show the younger players a thing or two.

He is a big, burly man – the sort who fits uncomfortably into any indoor scene and who wears a suit as if it was a straight-jacket. His element is the great outdoors. He needs the fresh air and he is never happier than when ploughing a straight furrow or bringing in the harvest with a pitchfork in his enormous, calloused hands.

Jethro, eldest son of Mabel and the late Ned Larkin, left the family home when he was still a young man and got a job in Dorset. When he came back to Ambridge, in 1966, he brought with him a wife and family. They live at Rickyard Cottage and he now works for Ambridge Farmers Ltd at Brookfield Farm, where he is right-hand man to Philip Archer.

Lizzie Larkin

Cooking is the favourite pastime of Mrs Lizzie Larkin – and it shows in the ample forms of her husband and daughter. Her style owes more, perhaps, to English Basic than Cordon Bleu, but her steak-and-kidney pudding is a mouth-watering dish that would grace any gourmet's table.

Her art was actually born out of necessity. After long hours on the farm, her husband Jethro was always ravenous when he got home and, like the good country wife she is, Lizzie has always seen it as her job to keep her man contented. When Jethro brought her to

Ambridge from her native Dorset, she didn't know anyone and, being a very shy woman, didn't make friends easily, so she spent more and more time in the kitchen. More recently, however, she joined the Women's Institute, and there she really came into her own at the regular produce sales where her home-made cakes and pastries are always best buys.

Mabel Larkin

Before her husband Ned died about eight years ago, Mrs Mabel Larkin was one of the brightest and most cheerful souls in Ambridge, and she was always bustling around the village with a ready smile for everyone. But her husband's death hit her very badly and she has become quiet and introvert. She is seldom seen these days and never goes to any of the social events.

She still works, and acting as housekeeper to one of the most recent newcomers, Mr Brian Aldridge, seems to take up most of her time. Her only other outings are to visit her sister in Hollerton and her son Jethro and his family at Rickyard Cottage.

Before Ned died, she used to work at the local market garden and she helped Doris Archer when she was still at Brookfield farmhouse. At one time she also acted as housekeeper to Hugo Barnaby when he lived at Glebe Cottage.

Arnold Lucas

When the squire and his family left Ambridge, they decided to keep their home, the Dower House, almost for sentimental reasons, but also because they weren't sure when they would want to come back. However, Mr Bellamy's business instincts were as sharp as ever and he decided to rent the house rather than let it lie empty. The new tenant is Mr Arnold Lucas, a retired solicitor, who has moved in but has hardly been seen by anyone in the village. Mrs Blossom, who kept house for the squire, also works for him but she isn't very forthcoming about who or what he is. He seems to want to live as a recluse and in many ways he couldn't have chosen a better place than Ambridge because the villagers are unlikely to interfere with his privacy.

Nora McAuley

The lilting Irish brogue of Nora McAuley has been a feature at 'The Bull' in Ambridge for ten years now, and she is still the most popular barmaid they have ever had in the pub. It hasn't been an easy ten years for Nora – she's had a broken engagement, an unhappy marriage and divorce, an affair with a married man, and a miscarriage – but she has shouldered her troubles with an Irish charm that seldom betrays bitterness.

She left her home near Belfast to come to Ambridge to join her fiancé, Paddy Redmond, who at the time worked for the Archers at Brookfield Farm. She settled into the village almost at once, and when Paddy decided to leave suddenly, she refused to go with him and broke off the engagement. It was only afterwards that she – and the rest of Ambridge – discovered that he had been the father of Jennifer Archer's illegitimate baby.

Although she didn't realise it at the time, she was on the rebound when she met Gregory Salt, who also worked at Brookfield, and within the year they became engaged, marrying the following year. The marriage lasted only four years and most of that time Nora was unhappy because of Gregory's lack of ambition. In the end it was he who decided to leave her, and when he did

Nora moved to live in at 'The Bull' and took on more responsibility by running the bed-and-breakfast side of the business.

But Nora is the sort of woman who needs a man around to mother or depend on according to her mood, and when she met George Barford, the new game-keeper, he so obviously needed mothering that she could hardly resist him. To most of the villagers he was just a miserable character with a chip on his shoulder, but it didn't take Nora long to discover that he had been an alcoholic who was desperately trying to fight it. He just seemed to want to be left on his own and he resented all Nora's efforts to help. In the end her per-sistance won the day, he was grateful for her friendship, and they started living together. After a stormy few months, she couldn't stand his moods and left him – only to discover that she was pregnant.

When he realised, George asked her to come back. He turned over a new leaf and was as excited as Nora about the baby. They were both broken-hearted when Nora had a miscarriage. It has, however, brought them much closer together and the future now looks a bit brighter for both.

Angus McLaren

For more than fifteen years Dr Angus McLaren has been ministering to the needs of Ambridge's sick and suffering. His battered old car, with the little black bag thrown carelessly in the back seat, is instantly recog-nised by everyone in the district and its appearance outside any house is an instant sign that someone is ill.

Something of a dour Scot, Dr McLaren is a very hard-working and conscientious man and his total devotion to his patients more than makes up for any lack of humour. Before coming to Ambridge, he was in practice in another rural district in the North of England and he therefore has long experience of coun-try medicine, which he says is vastly different from that practised in towns and cities. Farm work, for example, throws up different injuries and illnesses to factories; and country people are less prone to imaginary illnesses and are, he claims, better able to describe their symptoms.

Some people have suggested that he fall in line with many other doctors and start up a group practice or a medical centre, but Dr McLaren prefers to carry on as he always has done, giving personal attention to anyone and everyone who comes to his surgery or needs a visit from him.

Jennifer Macy

As Jennifer Archer, Mrs Macy made quite a name for herself in the literary world. She had her first short stories published while still a teenager and she was only twenty-two when one of her novels went into paperback and the best-sellers lists. Now, still only thirty, she's attempting a comeback with one thriller *(It's Murder)* on the bookstalls and another *(Feet of Clay)* due out soon.

If Mrs Macy's personal courage and determination have anything to do with it, she should soon be back among the best-sellers. She has had to battle against her youthful reputation as the black sheep of the Archer family, and recently her marriage has broken up, leaving her to look after her two children, Adam (8) and Deborah (5), singlehanded.

The oldest of the three children of Mrs Peggy Archer and the late Jack Archer, Jennifer first started going off the rails when her schooling was disrupted by her parents leaving Ambridge. She hated leaving behind all her friends at the village school, and when she was sent to a private school in Cornwall she wouldn't make friends with the children there. Then when the family moved back, she found herself teased unmercifully by her old friends because of the 'posh' uniforms she wore. This, on top of having to wear braces on her teeth, was all terribly traumatic for a sensitive young girl and it was hardly surprising when reaction set in and she started rebelling against any form of authority and discipline.

At home, her parents found her difficult to control and, when she was still not fifteen, they found she was going out with older boys, using make-up and wearing the then fashionable stiletto-heeled shoes. Her father tried to discipline her, but his own drinking habits left her scant regard for his admonitions.

For a while she seemed to settle down and she joined the local Young Farmers' Club, getting involved with country life a bit more. Then it was decided that she should take a domestic science course, with a view to helping run the restaurant side of her parents' pub. She had to go away for the course and as the college had no accommodation available, she went into digs and this soon led her into more trouble. After a wild party in her room, the landlady threw her out and there was a terrible rumpus with the college authorities and her father.

This incident, and the college's agreement that she could finish the course, made her pull herself together and it was at this time she started writing seriously. But even in her writing she was causing trouble: her first published story – in a woman's magazine – featured a loud-mouthed battleaxe of a woman who was clearly a model of her Aunt Laura! For the Archer family, however, the real scandal was yet to come. Jennifer was twenty-two when she set village tongues wagging by having an illegitimate child, and refusing to name the father.

The blow to the family – probably the best known in the whole county – was, to say the least, traumatic. At the time Jennifer was teaching infants at nearby Hollerton, and she had to quit instantly. Her father took it very badly and threatened to throw her out. Her maternal grandmother refused to speak to her, and most of her friends were angry that she wouldn't say who was the father, because it meant suspicion fell on most of the young men in the district. It turned out that the man was Paddy Redmond, a young Irishman who worked for her grandfather at Brookfield Farm. It didn't help matters that he had, only months earlier, brought his fiancée, Nora McAuley, over from Belfast to work as barmaid for the Archers at 'The Bull'. He left Ambridge – and Nora – shortly before the baby was born. Jennifer, too, left the village. When her son Adam was born, she went to Bristol and worked for about a year as a teacher.

When she returned to Ambridge, she met her husband-to-be, Roger, who was then running a book-shop in Borchester. He completely accepted the situation, and when they later married he adopted little Adam as his own child. Jennifer settled into married life with enthusiasm and energy. Between writing and looking after Adam, she helped Roger set up a new health-food business next door to his book-shop. They were idyllically happy – but not for long. In 1970 Adam was kidnapped! Jennifer recalls that it was like something out of one of her own novels and she simply could not believe it was happening to her.

The nightmare lasted for a week before the police found Adam safe. And during that seemingly-endless week of agony and soul-searching, she and Roger grew closer and closer together. The seal was set, everyone thought, on their relationship with the birth of their daughter Deborah on Christmas Eve that year.

Jennifer cannot explain exactly why, but only four years later it became apparent that there was some-thing wrong with the marriage. She had never got on very well with her mother-in-law and this had caused some tension with Roger, and then he gave up his business for a job that took him away from home a lot. She got fed up on her own in Borchester and took a part-time job in Ambridge, helping her mother with the book-keeping at Grey Gables Country Club. Then when she found the travelling backwards and forwards too difficult, she decided to stay in Ambridge – temporarily.

She has now made up her mind to stay on permanently, and although the future is uncertain she is determined to do her best for the children. Such responsibility could be just the spur she needs to get back among the best-sellers.

Johnnie Martin

Tom Forrest could not be prouder of young Johnnie Martin if he was his own son instead of just his foster child. Johnnie, who first went to live with the Forrests when he was nine, now works on Lord Felpersham's estate and seems set for a key job in forestry management.

When he left school, Johnnie worked for Ralph Bellamy, and even at that early stage he showed enough promise for Ralph to send him on a long training course in forestry. Later he went to the Felpersham estate for a further year's training but when that was completed he was asked to stay on permanently. He is engaged to a Felpersham girl and they plan to marry as soon as Johnnie knows about the new job that is in prospect.

Frank Mead

When Frank Mead died last year, it came as a blessed relief to his daughter Polly, and her husband Sid Perks. They had stopped visiting him at the mental hospital where he died, because each occasion had upset Polly so much. Then they spent the rest of the time feeling guilty for not going to see him.

Mr Mead used to run his own small-holding at Penny Hassett and he worked part-time for Ambridge farmer, Philip Archer. At that time he was regarded by most people as being just slightly dotty: he was always quoting from the Bible and denouncing those who drank alcohol. That was, in fact, the beginning of his illness, and it started to become apparent by the way he reacted so strongly when Polly began work at 'The Bull'.

His condition deteriorated rapidly and he was finally committed to the mental hospital after being caught causing fires around the village.

Lizzie Mead

Before her husband died Mrs Lizzie Mead lived in the hope that he would one day be released from the mental hospital and come back home to a normal life. She kept the old people's bungalow in which she lived just as he would have wanted it, with all his things around the place. She hasn't yet got used to being a widow, although she has, of course, lived alone for many years now, and she is terribly dependent on the moral support of her daughter and son-in-law.

Trina Muir

When Trina Muir first came to Ambridge, she brought with her a very large chip on her shoulder. It was there because of a riding accident that brutally cut short a promising show-jumping career and left her partially crippled.

An attractive young Scots girl, she still walks with a limp, but the chip seems lighter in the few years she has been in the village. She is co-director of, and helps to run, the local riding-school. Although all thoughts of competing again have been completely dispelled, she can now ride quite well, and being back working with horses has obviously helped her. In addition, of course, the natural friendliness of the country folk make it difficult to go on being resentful.

Her only disappointment locally was over one of her pupils at the riding-school, young Shula Archer. She thought Shula showed promise as a show-jumper and, when world champion Ann Moore confirmed her opinion and gave her some special coaching, she had visions of her championship ambitions being realised through Shula. But in the event, Shula decided against going on to become a professional.

Polly Perkins

Many people in Ambridge will simply look blank if you talk about Mrs Polly Perkins, or they may think you have made a mistake and actually mean Mrs Polly Perks, licensee at 'The Bull'. But mention 'Mrs P' and everyone will know at once that you are referring to the eccentric little Cockney woman who has lived in the village off and on for the past twenty-five years.

Mrs P first ventured out of London when her first husband died and she came on a short visit to her daughter and son-in-law, Peggy and Jack Archer. As mothers-in-law are wont to do, she decided to make the short stay into a longer stay, but even Jack Archer never imagined it would go on for quarter of a century!

As an 'unattached' lady, she soon became prey to Ambridge's own Casanova, Walter Gabriel, and it wasn't long before he had her entangled in his misadventures. She was persuaded to help with the novelty stall at the village fête, and she spent weeks making lavender bags that no one really wanted. Then the following year she was conned into acting as the fortune-teller but her own success terrified her: she gave dark warnings to young Christine Archer about an impending mishap – and Christine went out laughing and tripped over the tent peg!

When she eventually got wise to Walter, she was more than a match for him and, while she accepted his gift of a pony and trap, she very deftly kept him at more than arm's length. Nevertheless, Walter and the rest of the villagers were shocked when she announced her intention of marrying a second Mr Perkins – Arthur Perkins, who had been visiting Ambridge to work on the church's stained-glass windows. After the wedding, they both went back to live in London.

When Arthur had a heart attack in 1965, she brought him to a country nursing-home near Ambridge and she rented Rickyard Cottage. Her next exit was in high dudgeon and shock caused by her grand-daughter, Jennifer, having an illegitimate baby. It took her nearly a year to get over that and make her peace with Jennifer. But she did, and when Arthur died she came back yet again to live in Ambridge.

Walter Gabriel was still around and still making proposals. However, she has so far managed to resist him, and she has joined the Over-60s Club with a view, no doubt, to running her eye over the rest of the field.

Polly Perks

From a shy young barmaid, uncertainly pulling her first pint, Mrs Polly Perks has become the confident and charming landlady of Ambridge's famous country pub 'The Bull' – and all in less than ten years.

When Polly first worked at 'The Bull', she wasn't quite twenty-one and she didn't really know her martini from her bacardi. She was so shy that she blushed every time someone ordered a drink! But all the time she was learning the trade, never dreaming, of course, that she would one day be the boss.

Her husband Sid, whom she married when she was twenty-two, thinks he is the boss, but it is Polly who holds the licence and, in her subtle way, it is she who controls all the important decisions about running the pub. In fact, since their marriage she has been pushing

Sid in the right direction all the time.

She persuaded him to give up his job as a pig-man for a doubtful character called Brown, but he was sacked before he could do so and went to work in the local garage. Polly still wasn't too happy, and when she won £1000 on the Premium Bonds, she used it as the deposit on buying the village stores and post office, and became postmistress, hoping that Sid would help run the stores side of the business. But he went on working at the garage.

When she became pregnant, however, he did decide to give up at the garage and run the shop, but just before he started, there was an attempted robbery at the post office and Polly was attacked. She later had a miscarriage.

It was after her second pregnancy, and the birth of her daughter Lucy, that Peggy Archer offered the tenancy of 'The Bull'. Polly wanted to jump at the chance, but there was a problem: just as Sid couldn't become postmaster because of his youthful but criminal offences, nor could he become the licensee of a pub. Polly had to use all her wiles on Sid before he finally agreed to sell up the shop and move into 'The Bull'. Once there, she started developing the restaurant side, opening a new steak-bar and later a ploughman's bar, while she got Nora McAuley moving on the bed-and-breakfast business and Sid on the physical alterations!

Sid Perks

If the years he has spent in Ambridge have done little for Sid Perks's Birmingham accent, at least they have smoothed down some of the rough edges and tempered him into the cheerful, affable character he is now.

Sid could perhaps have been best described as a rough diamond when he spent a holiday at Grey Gables Country Club in 1963. He wasn't quite a tearaway, but he had been in a remand home for breaking and entering and some of his mates were set to be long-term thugs.

66

Oddly enough, the lure of a peaceful country life wasn't offered Sid by any of the natives but by another Brummie, Mr Jack Woolley, the boss of the country club. He obviously saw something of himself in the young Sid and took to him immediately. When Sid tipped him off that his club steward was on the fiddle he offered him a job and Sid became his chauffeur and general assistant.

After Sid married Polly, Mr Woolley asked them to run his recreation centre at Arkwright Hall, but the centre wasn't a success and it closed after a few months, leaving him out of work. He then had a series of jobs before finally he and Polly – with Mr Woolley's financial help – took over the village stores and post office. He was upset that his criminal record precluded him from becoming the new postmaster and he wouldn't work in the shop at all, preferring to keep on his job at the local garage, but when, one day, he did help in the stores, he enjoyed it so much that, when Polly became pregnant, he readily conceded defeat and took it on full-time.

Sid does everything with enthusiasm, and within weeks he was reorganising the shop lay-out, painting the frontage and running a mobile shop as a sideline. Between times, he still found the energy to re-form the village cricket team and set up an extensive fixture list. When he found the mobile shop idea wasn't financially worthwhile, he abandoned it and instead streamlined the stores, making it into a self-service shop.

Just as he had got things the way he wanted them, along came the offer of the tenancy of 'The Bull', and in the end he couldn't resist the temptation of another challenge. And running a country pub was a challenge, especially since he didn't have the experience, and it didn't go as well as Sid expected. In the second year business dropped off so badly that he decided drastic action was needed. He gave up his interest in the football team he'd been running and turned his full attention on 'The Bull'. He installed fruit machines, redecorated the bedrooms to increase the bed and breakfast trade, opened for morning coffees and afternoon teas, and created a new ploughman's bar. He also became a small-time travel agent by organising a coach trip to Holland and visits to events like Smithfield and the Royal Show. He would have liked to extend the premises and go for the motel trade but it proved too costly and he had to drop the idea.

His latest hobby-horse is the new bowling green which he created last year and is now carefully nursing towards its full lushness in time for the start of the bowls season.

Alice Peters

When her husband lost his job and his tied cottage, Mrs Peters jumped at the offer of becoming caretaker at Hollowtree Flats, because it would give them a roof over their heads – even if it was still 'tied'.

Sam Peters

Sam Peters had been cowman on the local estate farm for many years when his health broke down a couple of years ago. Ralph Bellamy had to ask him to leave his job and the cottage that went with it because, he said, he needed it for the new cowman.

Sam's pride was badly dented and he turned down the offers of other jobs – car-park attendant or caretaker – that Ralph had tried to arrange for him. Instead he found a job himself, as milk tester for Borchester Dairies.

John Poole

Dr John Poole, who joined Dr McLaren's practice in 1974, is a graduate of the same university – Edinburgh – but there are more than twenty-five years between the dates of their degrees. The relationship they have formed could almost be a product of A. J. Cronin out of Tannochbrae. The young Dr Poole is able to complement Dr McLaren's long experience in general medicine with his more recent training and awareness of new developments. It is a combination that works well in the interests of the village.

Ken Pound

Ken Pound successfully reared Friesians and Jerseys on his 150-acre dairy farm for many years. But he came unstuck when he decided to cross-breed the two in the hope of producing high-quality milk. However, being a good farmer, he has changed back to his old style and will recover his losses fairly quickly.

Mary Pound

While her husband has run his dairy herds, Mary Pound developed her own little business selling produce from the farm gate, and this was so successful that she is now in partnership in a farm shop with Carol Tregorran.

Maggie Price

Although she lives in Borchester, young Maggie Price spends most of her free time in Ambridge. She became friendly with Shula Archer and Neil Carter when they were at the technical college together. She is a shorthand-typist in a travel agency but she loves riding and is very keen to help with Shula's scheme for giving riding classes to disabled children.

Ernest Purdy

The tenant at Paunton Farm, Ernest Purdy is very interested in politics, and his first step towards the corridors of power was to stand for the Ambridge Parish Council in 1973. He was unsuccessful but undeterred and he is now studying the policies of the three main parties with a view to offering himself as a candidate for the next district council election.

Gloria Redding

No one knows why Mrs Gloria Redding goes on living in Ambridge. She lives in the Hollowtree Flats and is constantly telling anyone who will listen that she hates them, that she can't stand the village and doesn't even care for the country at large. She was, she says, never happier than when she and her husband were in the furniture business in her native Birmingham.

Philip Reynolds

It was his passionate interest in natural history and wildlife that made Philip Reynolds give up a very good job in industry and come back to Ambridge as warden of the Field Centre.

Philip was brought up in Ambridge, but while he was at university his father got a new job in the South and the family moved away. After graduating he joined them and went into industry. But when his fiancée, a Penny Hassett girl, told him about the vacancy at the Field Centre he jumped at the chance of getting back to the country. He got the job, they married and moved in to Arkwright Hall.

Ian Robertson

After more than twenty-five years of tending the sick animals around Ambridge, Ian Robertson is taking life a little easier these days and lets his son shoulder most of the strain of being a country vet.

Mr Robertson, like so many in his profession, is a

Scotsman but he settled in England just after the war and his accent is barely discernible. While he likes to spend more and more time fishing and golfing, he still has no intention of retiring for at least another ten years.

Gregory Salt

It took Gregory Salt only three years to realise he had made a mistake in marrying Nora McAuley, barmaid at 'The Bull'. Although he had previously had his own small farm, he was a stockman when they married and Nora had greater ambitions for him than he had himself. For a quiet life and a bit more money he took a job as a milkman in Borchester. When that didn't satisfy Nora, he started seeing another woman and the marriage was on the rocks. It finally floundered and he left to live with the other woman in Borchester, while Nora arranged the divorce.

Andrew Sinclair

Now acting as agent for an absent landlord, Andrew Sinclair has been managing farm and estate business for Ambridge landowners since 1962. Another of the village's Anglo-Scots, he came down from his native Perthshire to run Charles Grenville's farm interests and, when Mr Grenville died, he decided to go home and accept his cousin's offer of running the family's farm. The company that took over the Grenville estate did, however, make him an excellent counter-offer and he stayed on and married a local girl.

He survived other changes in the estate's ownership and, when Ralph Bellamy decided to retire but retain 1000 acres of land, he was his first choice as agent. Now he has sole responsibility for maintaining the estate.

Dorothy Sinclair

Her husband's decision to stay in Ambridge delighted Mrs Dorothy Sinclair because she is a local girl and she didn't want to leave all her family and friends. Mrs

Sinclair, who is slightly crippled, used to run a home hairdressing scheme and did dressmaking before managing a gown shop in Borchester for a while. She gave up work after her marriage and the birth of her son, Hamish, who is now nearly ten.

Nancy Smith

Young Nancy Smith is one of a rare breed today – a girl who is happy to be in service just like her mother and grandmother before her. She is maid to the Tregorrans and she seems to enjoy her work there, although it has to be said that – unlike her mother and grandmother – she has the advantage of almost every labour-saving gadget imaginable, including a dish-washer.

She also gets plenty of free time to do whatever she wants. She's happy enough with the wages, too, because, living in as she does, she gets free board and lodging and she can use her wages to buy the latest fashions and make-up.

Emily Spenlow

Mrs Emily Spenlow is a splendidly dotty woman who insists that her dead husband keeps in touch with her 'through the spirits'. She is the source of endless amusement to the village although everyone is careful not to poke fun at her – just in case she is right.

Peter Stevens

The younger of the two boys fostered by Tom and Pru Forrest, Peter Stevens is the village's mechanic. He works at the local garage and does all the maintenance for Ambridge Farmers Ltd and other local farms.

While he was a teenager, Peter caused Tom a great deal of embarrassment by getting involved in poaching. Luckily for him, Pru was able to convince Tom that it was only a schoolboy prank. Since then, Peter has changed his ways, and he now belongs to an 'action group' which aims at helping old people.

Helen Summers

Ambridge is lucky to have Mrs Helen Summers working for Dr McLaren. She is a fully qualified state-registered nurse with long experience in a big London teaching hospital. She came back to the district when her husband moved to Borchester from London to take over his company's Midland branch.

Ian Sylvane

Ian Sylvane, the *Borchester Echo* reporter who helped Mrs Doris Archer publish her diaries, has recently been promoted to assistant editor with responsibility for all the village coverage by the paper.

Emily Tarbutt

Emily Tarbutt is the cousin of a former vicar of Ambridge but she had never been to the village before 1969, when she became companion to Mrs Agatha Turvey.

Mrs Turvey actually wanted a cook-companion, but Emily doesn't like cooking although she loves gardening. So they compromised: Mrs Turvey looks after the kitchen and Emily looks after the garden.

Elsie Timms

Mrs Elsie Timms is another of the farm workers' wives who find they cannot make ends meet on their husband's wages. Her husband works on the Bellamy estate and they have a service flat at low rental, but Elsie earns extra cash by helping Doris Archer with the housework at Glebe Cottage and by doing cleaning work at 'The Bull.'

George Timms

It was ill health that forced George Timms to resign as clerk to the Parish Council, a job he'd held for many years. He was succeeded by Haydn Evans. Mr Timms, a retired schoolmaster, still takes some interest in the council business and he is always ready with advice for Haydn, but only if asked. He knows there is nothing worse than having your predecessor looking over your shoulder all the time.

Arthur Tovey

The Manager of Carol Tregorran's orchards, Arthur Tovey spends little time in Ambridge. He is a bachelor and a stock-car enthusiast, and every spare moment he has he uses to dash off to some meeting or another. He no longer races himself, but he does own two cars which he lends to young drivers in return for keeping them tuned and in racing condition.

Joe Tozer

He would describe himself as a Man of the Road, but those who know him better recognise Joe Tozer as an old scrounger. Someone in the village must have been generous to him at some time because Ambridge is now very much on his touring map. He turns up regularly offering to do odd jobs, but is usually horrified if anybody asks him to do any work – and that is the best way to get him to move on.

Carol Tregorran

It is difficult for the outsider to determine just what it is that drives Mrs Carol Tregorran so relentlessly forward. It could be cold-blooded ambition or simply an excess of restless energy: whichever, she works at a pace that would leave most of today's businessmen exhausted. And she does it so effortlessly that it doesn't detract from the care she gives her husband and young family.

No one had yet coined the phrase 'Women's Lib.' when she barged her way into the predominantly male world of smallholdings and market gardens and, while still in her teens, successfully ran a small business in her native Surrey. She took Ambridge by storm in 1954. She bought a vacant smallholding from Dan Archer,

converted it into a market garden, put his eldest son, Jack, in as foreman, and then persuaded a very hard-headed businessman, George Fairbrother, to join her as a partner.

That is how she intended to go on and that *is* how she has gone on. With Mr Fairbrother she expanded the business and moved on to some of his land. When that land changed hands and Charles Grenville became the new owner, he wasn't interested in the market garden and she had a very difficult time with him. But falling back on her feminine charms, she even did that successfully – and Charles eventually ended up marrying her.

It may have been from her parents that she inherited some of her restlessness. They were both artists and had never got round to marrying. In fact they parted when she was only two, and she was left to be brought up by her mother's cousin, James Grey, and his wife, until they were both killed during the blitz. She was then farmed out to another relative in Surrey.

She slowed down for the first time in 1962 when her first child, Richard, was born. She was idyllically happy and it may be that she would have settled down to simply being a wife and mother if it hadn't been for a tragic accident. Charles was taking Janet Tregorran home after a visit when the car crashed. Janet was killed and Charles lost a leg. It was particularly traumatic because she and Janet's husband John (whom she later married) had been very close before her own marriage to Charles.

Just as it seemed as if she and Charles were adjusting to his disability, he went to America and died there suddenly, six months after the accident. A lesser woman might have cracked. Carol didn't. She set about settling Charles's business affairs and getting a trust arranged to run the estate on behalf of Richard, who had inherited it. Two years later, when John Tregorran proposed, she found herself faced with the most difficult decision in her life, and it took her a long time before she said yes.

Once remarried, she went back to business and, just before she had her daughter, Anna Louise, she bought a fifty-acre orchard. This time the new baby's arrival caused only the barest slowing down, and within months she was buying new glasshouses, trying out the latest driverless tractor, and going into the health-food business with a shop in Borchester.

More recently, she has put down a vineyard, started a pick-your-own-fruit scheme, and gone into partnership with a local farmer in a farm-shop. Her energy seems boundless and sometimes John gets a bit worried about what she may get up to next. But whatever it might be, he will be fairly certain that she will make a success of it.

John Tregorran

When John Tregorran wakes up in the morning and opens his bedroom window to the crisp, clean country air and looks out over the rolling meadows, he often wonders what his life might have been like if he hadn't won the football pools twenty-five years ago. Instead of a large and comfortable country house, he could still be living on some crowded university campus, waiting vainly for a head of department's job or maybe even a chair. And when he thinks like that, he is more grateful than ever that luck was on his side.

He won £75,000, left his job, bought an old gypsy caravan and just faded away from the redbrick university where he had been a lecturer. On his way through Ambridge – although he didn't even know it was Ambridge at the time – the old caravan broke a wheel and he had to stop for a while to get it repaired.

He got a very poor welcome in the village because he was thought to be one of the gypsies who had been causing trouble in the district. He was even accused of horse-stealing. Luckily, however, the confusion was cleared up and the villagers became quite friendly. Which was just as well because the real gypsies burned his caravan and left him homeless.

He moved into 'The Bull', and it was there that he first came to grips with local history. With time on his hands, he browsed through old books and became more and more interested. When he was able to tell one of the farmers that some old foundations discovered on his land were of the original manor house, he was well and truly hooked and decided to stay on a little longer. By then he was more or less accepted in the village and, when he was offered a partnership in a nursing home, he jumped in with both feet. It did prove to be the deep end and his erstwhile partner later disappeared owing him money. With this interest in history, however, he had been finding interesting bits and pieces of antique jewellery, furniture and so on. From there it was only a matter of time before he bought an antique shop in Borchester.

Having lost his horse-drawn caravan, John had bought a new means of transport – a motor-bike on which he used to roar through the country lanes. It was on one of those escapades that – quite literally – he ran into the girl who was eventually to become his wife. She was then Miss Carol Grey and she was driving her car at the time he smashed into it.

Neither was badly hurt and they quickly became friends, but when John first proposed to her she treated the whole thing as a joke. That upset John, and he carried a torch for her for many years after that – even after she married Charles Grenville. When he did get over her, he became engaged to the district nurse, Janet Sheldon, and they married in 1963. But four months later there was the most gruesome twist of fate. Janet had been visiting the Grenvilles and Charles gave her a lift home. On the way there was an accident in which she was killed and Charles was seriously injured. He too died six months later.

It was all too much for John and he went to Spain for a long holiday. When he came back, he threw himself into hard work: he formed a partnership with Walter Gabriel for making rocking-chairs, and another with Roger Travers-Macy in selling antiquarian books.

In the end, however, nothing else would work and he turned again to Carol and asked her to marry him. When she agreed, they married nearly fifteen years after he had first proposed. At long last he found peace of mind.

Since then he has diversified his interest, opening a museum, organising a festival to mark the 1000th anniversary of the church, and lecturing in America. His most recent lecture-tour there caused some domestic problems, because it lasted much longer than expected – nearly seven months. Carol was particularly upset when there were some difficulties at her son's boarding school over his stealing. John, as his step-father, didn't think he would be able to help and decided against coming back. But he changed his mind and, flying home ahead of schedule, went to see the boy at the school. He was delighted with the result of his visit because it had clearly given the lad quite a lift out of his depression.

It also made him firmly resolve that in future there will be no more prolonged absences from Ambridge.

Betty Tucker
Before she married, young Betty Tucker lived on her family's smallholding in Derbyshire and there she saw

how much could be eked out of the tiniest scrap of land. She is using her experience to very good effect in Ambridge where her cottage has a pocket-handkerchief-size garden. She did try to breed sheepdogs from a pedigree pair she got from her father, but that proved uneconomic and instead she now keeps bees and goats. She already sells the goats' milk to a health-food shop and will no doubt find a ready market for the honey when it's ready.

Mike Tucker
Mike Tucker didn't exactly make himself popular with local farmers when his first action on arriving in Ambridge was to revive the branch of the agricultural workers' union. His intention was simply to ensure that the farmworkers were not being exploited, but his tub-thumping manner caused a bit of ill-feeling and it didn't help when he seemed to be looking for test cases in which to pit the union against the employers, presumably as part of a drive for new members.

There is, of course, another side to his union activities and he does a series of lectures on farm safety and how the farmworker can protect himself from accidents.

Agatha Turvey
Putting up with Walter Gabriel as a partner is quite an achievement, but Mrs Turvey went one better a few years back – she kicked him out of the business because he wasn't pulling his weight!

Mrs Turvey is a splendid old lady who lives with an elderly companion and a cat called Tiddles. Nothing can intimidate her and, when the council's road plans reduced the size of her garden, she demanded and got ample compensation.

Deirdre Underwood
An attractive young redhead, Deirdre Underwood was one of many girls who fell for the dashing charm of

Tony Archer in his sports-car days. She lived with her mother at Hollowtree Flats and, though very well off, they were nouveau riche and it showed. They left Ambridge because it wasn't quite grand enough, but Deirdre did come back to visit Tony and she tried unsuccessfully to lure him to Wales for a weekend.

Bobby Waters
When Ralph Bellamy took over Brigadier Winstanley's estate, it looked as if one of the victims of the subsequent reorganisation would be tenant-farmer Bobby Waters. But he became manager of Bellamy's new 120-cow units and, although he could have given up because of back trouble, he decided to continue in the job when Bellamy retired.

Any fears that Bobby had that he would find it difficult to take orders after having been his own boss for so long were soon dispelled. Bellamy seldom interfered once the units were working properly and of course Bobby works entirely on his own.

Mary Weston
Mary Weston, a very pretty twenty-two-year-old, came to Ambridge as a travelling farm secretary – and nearly stayed to become Mrs Tony Archer. She was actually engaged to Tony but after a holiday on her own in Majorca she changed her mind and broke it off, just a few months before the wedding was planned. She later married her boss and now lives in Borchester.

Joby Woodford
When Ralph Bellamy brought in Joby Woodford as his forestry expert, he couldn't have picked a better man. On the surface Joby is slow-witted and a bit ponderous but there is little he doesn't know about timber growing, and he has the reputation of being the best woodsman in the county.

He is a very shy man, and this was one of the reasons

he didn't marry until late in life. But he reckons he did well to wait because when he did wed it was Martha Lily, widow and best cook in Ambridge, who became his wife.

For all his shyness and gentleness Joby is also a very tough and determined character. When they married, Martha worked the petrol pumps at the garage and did some household chores for one or two people. Joby didn't like that and it wasn't long before Martha gave both up, and got a better job in the village shop. It was the same when young Neil Carter came to lodge with them. Joby felt he had to keep a fatherly eye on the lad but Neil resented that and tried to rebel. Patient but firm, Joby persevered and in the end Neil accepted and even welcomed the discipline.

In his own job, too, Joby's determination to do well has paid off. When Ralph Bellamy went away he left 1000 acres in the capable hands of Joby.

Martha Woodford

There is little that happens in Ambridge that Martha Woodford doesn't know about. From her privileged position in the village stores and post office, she can actually see all the activity around the green, but, more importantly, her friendly nature makes her privy to countless secrets.

It's to Martha that those folk who can't find a sympathetic ear elsewhere turn, when something is bothering them. And they can do so because they know that it won't go further. Not that Martha is averse to gossip. She's not. She likes nothing better than a good chinwag about what Walter Gabriel has been up to or who has been seen with whom and where! But she knows about loyalty, and when there's a need for it nobody is stauncher than her.

Young Neil Carter knows that to his advantage. Some time after he went to lodge with her and Joby, he got involved with the police over drugs. He told Martha

81

that the drugs had been planted on him at a party and she never for a moment disbelieved him, not even when he was put on probation.

Joby is her second husband. Her first, who died about fifteen years ago, had been the postman at Penny Hassett for nearly thirty years. She lived there before marrying Joby, and she used to cycle across to Ambridge on a battered old bike so that she could work part-time at the Field Centre at Arkwright Hall. Then she did some general housework around the village and operated the petrol pumps at the garage.

She was a bit taken aback when Joby asked her to give up these jobs because he thought they were a bit unseemly for a woman like her. She soon realised, of course, that this was quite a compliment from him and she did as he asked. It was then that she first worked at the stores part-time, and that gave her plenty of time to show Joby what a good cook she was and how wicked she was at making the most potent wines from the most innocent ingredients!

When the Coopers, who had run the shop and post office previously, left suddenly, Martha persuaded the owner, Jack Woolley, to let her take over. He was very reluctant but he did agree in the end – just as Martha knew all along. He has never had any cause for regret, nor the villagers any cause for complaint. Martha runs things with a mixture of efficiency and friendliness that everyone appreciates.

Jack Woolley

Any fears that the villagers might have had about Jack Woolley's country-park idea turning Ambridge into a sort of rural Blackpool have been well and truly dispelled. Today everyone talks with delight about the way he has used and even enhanced the natural environment. He has developed a beautiful park that allows the townsman to enjoy all the joys of the country-

side without creating problems for the countryman.
And for many he has turned the clock back to a gentler
age, by reopening the old railway track and running a
steam service for visitors. The sight of the old loco
snorting its way through the summer sunshine gladdens
many a heart, and revives memories of happier days.

Instead of filling the park with attractions like the
Golden Mile's raucous tinsel, he turned to give Nature
a hand in providing her own attractions. He has stocked
the park with deer; he has added geese and swans to the
wildfowl reserve; and he has opened a fish-hatchery.

For Jack it's part of a dream come true. Ever since he
came to Ambridge from the industrial smog of Birmingham, he has been captivated by the English countryside
and has wanted to share his enjoyment with others.
Now he is doing just that.

It was in 1962 that he first arrived in Ambridge as the
new owner of Grey Gables Country Club. He retained
all his business interests and rather regarded the club as
an investment that also allowed him some respite from
the pressures of industrial life. He had been brought up
in the back streets of Birmingham and, as he puts it,
dragged himself up by his boot-laces to make enough
money to be able to do as he pleased. Self-made men
are not, of course, the most popular people on earth,
and with his abrasive personality and obvious wealth,
Ambridge didn't welcome him with open arms. But he
gradually overcame all the natural reserve as his sheer

enjoyment of the rural life became more and more obvious.

Some of that rubbed off on Sid Perks, now at 'The Bull'. Sid, another Brummie, was a guest at Grey Gables and Jack liked him so much that he persuaded him to stay on to work as his chauffeur. As he became more involved in the social life of the village, he began to wind up his business interests, and he eventually put one of his staff in complete charge of his London office. This left him free to open a golf course at the club, buy a little shop in Borchester, become part-owner of the local paper, the *Borchester Echo*, and take over the shooting rights on the local estate.

About the same time he also remarried. His first wife had died several years before he came to Ambridge, and he married a local widow, Valerie Trentham, who had a young daughter. Sadly, the marriage was never really happy, and within a year it was beginning to crack, although he did get on well with Valerie's daughter, Hazel. In fact he later adopted her, even though his wife left him.

During his domestic trouble, he kept himself very much to himself and wasn't seen around the village for quite a long time. But when he came to terms with the situation, he was soon bustling about with his usual enthusiasm. He bought the village shop and post office, and started to develop the country park. He put so much effort into his schemes that it affected his health and he was ordered to rest by his doctor. Although he didn't actually rest much, he did cut out all his interests outside Ambridge.

In 1973 he was brutally attacked during a robbery at Grey Gables and his injuries, which probably caused a later heart attack, were serious enough to keep him in hospital for several weeks. He had taken on Peggy Archer as his personal assistant and she lived in at Grey Gables. She helped nurse him through his illness and divorce, and he asked her to marry him when the decree became absolute. He was very disappointed when she turned him down, and even more so when she felt it necessary to leave Grey Gables.

He had another setback when Hazel decided to leave Ambridge and find a job in London. So, just as he was when he came in 1962, Jack Woolley is alone. But the difference now is that he has many good friends in the village, and he has an almost passionate love of the countryside. Despite his past worries in his personal life, he regards himself as a lucky man to have worked his way from the narrow suburban streets to the wide-open spaces of Ambridge.

Who Was Who

Like any community, Ambridge sees its fair share of change, and in a quarter of a century people die, retire, marry, change their job, or simply get fed up and strike out for pastures new. Here we list some of the folk who have done some of these things and who are no longer players on the Ambridge stage.

Jess Allard
Jess Allard was one of three farmers who amalgamated the dairy side of their farms to form Ambridge Dairy Farmers Ltd in 1961. When he died soon afterwards, his sons – Joe and Rex – sold out to Philip Archer and left Ambridge.

Grace Archer
Young Grace Archer hadn't even got used to her new surname when she died. Just five short months after her wedding to Philip Archer and six days before her twenty-fifth birthday, she was killed in a tragedy that more than twenty years later still leaves its scar on Ambridge.

Grace was the only child of George Fairbrother, very wealthy businessman and landowner. He had doted on her and tried to shelter her from most of life's pressures, leaving her free to indulge her sporting interests which were mainly riding and playing tennis. It was a comfortable life for this beautiful young girl, but to it she added purpose when she married. Philip Archer was an ambitious young farmer, and together they planned to revolutionise the British agricultural industry.

They had also made a much more personal plan – to

start a family, and it was that decision they were celebrating when they went out to dinner at the Grey Gables Country Club. It was a pleasant evening and Grace and Philip felt that they had everything to live for. But within an hour Grace was dying in her husband's arms, as an ambulance rushed her vainly to hospital.

She had been trapped by falling timbers while trying to rescue her horses from the blazing stables. She had discovered the fire in the stables attached to the country club, when she had gone out to the car to look for an ear-ring she had dropped. Over the years since then, one of the most common phrases heard around the village is: 'If only Grace hadn't dropped that ear-ring . . .'

Jack Archer

After a life plagued by illness and failure, Jack Archer died in 1972 in a hospital far from his native Ambridge. He was fifty. The elder son of Dan and Doris Archer, he lived most of his life in the shadow of someone else's success and, as the years went by, that seemed to make him more and more bitter. It probably started when he went into the army during the last war.

He was just eighteen, and the war two years old, when he was called up. He was very much the country bumpkin alongside the smart city boys and he naturally turned to the one other countryman in his unit, Barney Lee from Cornwall. The two became good friends, but while Barney was a good soldier, Jack was mediocre. He seemed to have two left feet when it came to marching drill, and he could hardly find the target at rifle practice. He didn't mind the ribald comments of the NCOs and his other mates, but he hated it when Barney joined in.

In the end, however, the army did make a man of him and it also provided him with a wife. But back in Civvy Street after the war he brought his new bride,

87

Peggy, to Ambridge and a smallholding that never stood comparison with his father's very well-run farm. In desperation he decided to start again, well away from what he thought was the critical gaze of his family. He joined his old army pal, Barney Lee, in Cornwall. That didn't work either, and within a year he brought Peggy and the children back to Ambridge, where he took a job with his father at Brookfield.

Then he became licensee of 'The Bull' and headed yet again for further failure and trouble. He started drinking heavily, the brewery took away his licence but transferred it to his wife, and he had a breakdown that ended with him in a mental hospital.

He never fully recovered from that and for the next twenty years he was dogged by self-inflicted illnesses and bouts of heavy gambling. He found it more and more difficult to cope with his family, especially when his elder daughter, Jennifer, had an illegitimate child. After that his drinking got even heavier, and in 1971 he went into a clinic in Scotland. He never came back.

John Archer

While his eldest brother Dan stayed in Ambridge to run the family farm, John Archer left to make a new life for himself in Canada. After many years of struggle, he was successful and also married a very beautiful French girl. He went into the oil business and his company had an agency in London, but he has seldom been seen in Ambridge over the fifty and more years since he left.

Ted Arnold

For a period in the 1960s he was manager of the market garden, but he didn't think the job was big enough for him, so he left to find another in a different part of the country.

Amos Atkins

Amos was an old tenant-farmer on the Manor Estate

who later had a smallholding next to Brookfield Farm.
He died suddenly in 1957.

Audrey Atkins
She was Amos's niece and acted as his housekeeper until
his death, when she left the district.

Freda Banham
Mrs Banham was the last headmistress at the village
school. She took over in 1971, but left two years later
when the school was closed.

Hugo Barnaby
Hugo Barnaby, who lived in America, came to Ambridge to visit his cousin, John Tregorran, and liked the
village so much that he stayed on for a couple of years.
He wrote a book, which he dedicated to the villagers,
and set up a rural arts centre at Nightingale Farm. He
went back to America, and the arts centre was closed
last year.

Badger Barrett
Badger was a former huntsman for the squire who
worked at the local stables. He died in 1960.

Betty Barrett
She was a quiet, houseproud woman whose husband,
Fred, left her in 1968.

Fred Barrett
Fred was a small but important farmer in Ambridge.
He was chairman of the local NFU and he combined
with Jess Allard and Dan Archer to form Ambridge
Dairy Farmers Ltd. When he retired, he left his wife
and went to run a grocery shop in Borchester.

Albert Bates
He was Ambridge's policeman from 1964 until 1967,

when he was promoted and moved back to Borchester.

Nancy Beard
Mrs Beard came to the village as nanny to the Bellamy child but she was so strict and formal that even the Squire sacked her after a few weeks.

Ronnie Beddoes
At one time, Ronnie Beddoes was the temporary manager at 'The Bull', and he moved on to work at Grey Gables Country Club where he was very popular with the guests. He left for greater things in the late 1960s.

Jim Benson
He worked for the late George Fairbrother, but was sacked for insulting Mrs Fairbrother although he later got his job back. He left Ambridge in 1955.

Susan Blake
She was the fourteen-year-old who, a few years back, won the hearts of the villagers after she was caught trying to steal a hen. She had been looking after her sick mother and the hen was to have been their Christmas dinner. The locals reacted by clubbing together and buying the family an enormous hamper.

Sue Brent
Sue Brent brought the latest in hair styles to Ambridge in 1965 when she was barmaid at 'The Bull'. Her beehive hair-do and her Californian Poppy perfume lingered in local memory long after she departed in 1966.

Charles Brown
He came to Ambridge and took over the tenancy of Paunton Farm and bred pigs. But this turned out to be a 'front' for the gang involved in the mailbag robbery in the 1960s.

Fay Brown
She lived at Paunton Farm as Charles Brown's wife.

Josephine Bryant
She was secretary in Charles Grenville's estate office but left for another job in Borchester in 1963.

Geoff Bryden
He was Ambridge's village bobby from 1955 until his promotion as sergeant took him back to Borchester in 1964.

Norris Buckland
The Rev. Norris Buckland was priest-in-charge at the parish church for about a year before going back to London in 1956.

Amy Butler
Amy was one of the barmaids at 'The Bull' for nearly ten years. She left in 1969 to work at a Borchester hotel.

Marjorie Butler
She worked for Philip Archer in his pig-breeding unit for a couple of years up to 1957.

Alan Carey
He was a young ex-soldier who came to Ambridge as a guest of the Lawson-Hopes to try to get over his experiences in the Korean war, where he saw his twin brother burned alive in a tank.

Elsie Catcher
Miss Catcher was headmistress of the village school for sixteen years and, when she retired in 1967, they threatened to close the school, but a vigorous campaign won a stay of execution.

David Cavendish
Dr Cavendish ran a health clinic and persuaded John Tregorran to join him in a partnership. But then he disappeared owing John money.

Harry Cobb
He was a general handyman around the village, doing odd jobs for anyone who would pay. He suffered from bronchitis and left to go south.

George Coleman
George was an assistant gamekeeper to Tom Forrest. He left the district and moved to Staffordshire in 1963.

Angela Cooper
The daughter of George Cooper, she worked for a short time in the village post office but she ran off with Gwyn Evans, got married, and emigrated to Canada.

Bess Cooper
She was the wife of Simon Cooper, a farmworker at Brookfield.

George Cooper
He was an ex-railwayman who was brought to Ambridge by Jack Woolley to drive his steam engine in the country park. As that wasn't a full-time job, he put him in to run the village stores. He left when his daughter ran off.

Simon Cooper
Simon worked for Dan Archer at Brookfield for many years but retired in 1958 and lived on in the village until he died.

Dick Corbey
He was temporary manager at 'The Bull' for a short

period in 1972 but ran off with some of the takings and stock. He was caught and taken to court.

Mike Daly
He was a young Irishman who wrote quite good thrillers but had pretensions of greater things. He wanted to be a poet, but no one would publish his work. He left Ambridge in 1956.

Bob Daniels
Bob was the garage mechanic in Ambridge for many years before leaving to manage a petrol station in Hollerton.

David Escott
Mr Escott arrived in Ambridge with great ideas of selling his services as a design consultant to the landed gentry. He only managed to con Mrs Peggy Archer before he was rumbled. He left suddenly in 1974.

Dylan Evans
One of Haydn Evans's two sons, he stayed at Ambridge only briefly in 1973.

Gwyn Evans
He was Haydn Evans's other son, and it was for him that his father bought Willow Farm. But he wasn't very keen on farming and, when he fell in love with young Angela Cooper from the post office, they just ran away and got married. He is now living in Canada and working in a shoe shop.

George Fairbrother
Mr Fairbrother, father of Mrs Grace Archer who died in the stables fire in 1955, was a very wealthy business-man who owned a lot of land around Ambridge. He was a widower but had remarried. He upset most of the village with his project to mine ironstone, and there was

a great row about who owned the mineral rights to certain parcels of land. When he was forced to abandon the scheme, he was furious and threatened to sell up all his land and clear out, but Grace and one or two of the villagers persuaded him to stay. He died two years after his daughter, in 1957.

Helen Fairbrother
George Fairbrother's second wife, she sold up her interests in Ambridge, when he died, and went to live in Kenya.

Helen Fairlie
Mrs Fairlie was housekeeper and chauffeuse to Mrs Laura Archer. But she lost her confidence in driving after a minor accident and decided to find another job in Borchester.

Rita Flynn
A flighty Irish girl, she worked in the local bakery for Doughy Hood for a short period. She left in 1960.

Robin Freeman
He was warden at the Field Centre at Arkwright Hall but, after having domestic problems, he left to take up a lecturing post at a redbrick university in 1974.

Zoe Freeman
Robin's wife, she created difficulties in the marriage by going out with other men, and she eventually left him.

Bert Garland
Bert was a tenant farmer in Ambridge for many years. but after a very bad harvest he decided to pack it in and left the land altogether. With his wife Annie, he is now living up North.

Denise Garonne
A very elegant French lady, Madame Garonne came to the village with Charles Grenville as his housekeeper, but after only a short time she left to go home to France.

Debbie Glover
Debbie was one of the young girls who came from Borchester to work in the local market garden, but she didn't stay long and left in 1957.

Frances Graham
Frances was the attractive young librarian who ran a mobile service for the villages around Borchester. She was promoted in 1974 and took charge of the branch library at Hollerton.

Jimmy Grange
He spent two years as an apprentice with Dan Archer before moving to another farm in East Anglia in 1962. He is remembered as the village's first pop-singer. He bought himself a guitar and entertained at the local Young Farmers' Club.

Michele Gravencin
Michele's good looks caused many a young heart to flutter when she was *au pair* to Jill and Phil Archer. Tony Archer was one of the most disappointed when she went back to France in 1972, although she had been Gordon Armstrong's girl friend!

Ginger Green
Ginger, who despite his nickname didn't have red hair, worked for Philip Archer when he was running the poultry unit for George Fairbrother. He left in 1953.

Charles Grenville
Charles Grenville moved to Ambridge in 1959 when he bought the local estate from the previous squire's widow.

He married Carol Grey (now Tregorran) and they had a son Richard. Charles was driving the car in which John Tregorran's wife Janet was killed. He himself lost a leg in the accident, and died six months later while on a visit to America.

Harvey Grenville
The cousin of Charles, Harvey Grenville worked for the company that ran the estate after Charles's death. He was sacked when Ralph Bellamy bought the land, and he and his wife Ann then left Ambridge in rather a huff.

Eric Harvey
Dr Eric Harvey was the much-loved local GP who retired in 1952 and went to live at the seaside. He died a few years ago.

Diana Hood
Diana, one of three daughters of Betty and Percy Hood, worked in the poultry unit, too. Her sister Margaret worked for the hunt. They left when the family moved back north in 1959. Her other sister Joan stayed and married Nigel Burton.

Doughy Hood
Doughy's nickname gives his trade away. He was Ambridge's baker for ten years and, since he moved away on retiring in 1968, he is still a regular visitor.

Percy Hood
Percy and his wife Betty ran a smallholding in the village for many years. He died of a heart attack not long after he retired and went back north in 1959.

Herbert Johnson
Mr Johnson, an agricultural contractor and father of

Paul Johnson, died in 1957. His widow Hilda retired to live in Bournemouth.

Sid Jones

Sid was Ambridge's own burglar. He had been breaking into local houses for years before finally being caught in 1959. He was put away for a long stretch and, though it's doubtful if he learned his lesson, he never reappeared.

Lady Isobel Lander

Lady Isobel, niece of Brigadier Winstanley, inherited his estate in 1971 but decided to sell up rather than try to run it herself. She stayed in London and sold the land to Ralph Bellamy.

Bob Larkin

Bob was the unfortunate victim in the shooting incident which led to Tom Forrest being charged with murder. He was the brother of Ned Larkin.

Ned Larkin

Ned, a tough old countryman, was a farm-worker with Dan Archer until his death in 1960. His widow Mabel and son Jethro still live in the village.

David Latimer

The Rev. David Latimer was Vicar of Ambridge for five years before his death in 1973 after a long illness. His widow, Hester, left the village but is still an occasional visitor.

Tessa Latimer

Tessa was the Vicar's daughter. She left Ambridge in 1971 to join the probation service.

Clive Lawson-Hope

He was the squire's nephew who stayed in the Big House

in the early fifties and for a time courted Grace Fair-brother – unsuccessfully. He went to Kenya in 1953.

George Lawson-Hope

Squire Lawson-Hope was really the last of the old-style squires. He was the biggest landowner in the district and at one time almost everyone in the village was either his tenant or his employee. He had inherited the land and the title from his father, after his two older brothers had been killed in the First World War. He and his wife, Letty, were both very popular and were regarded by many of the villagers as friends – quite a feat even in the fifties. They both died in 1958.

John Martin

John Martin was one of the farmers who got fed up with the uphill struggle. He sold Bull Farm in 1974 and emigrated.

Jane Maxwell

Jane's blonde hair and soft, West-country accent made her one of the village's most popular girls. She worked on the Fairbrother farm until she went back to her home town, Bath, in 1952.

Alice Merryman

A bitter spinster, Miss Merryman was Jack Woolley's secretary until he discovered she had been writing anonymous letters. She was sacked and disappeared from the village.

John Michaels

Dr Michaels was the young GP who came to join Dr McLaren's practice, but after a trial period in 1973 he left to find a better position.

Lester Nicholson

He was the Canadian air-force pilot who swept Lilian

Archer off her feet in 1969. After a fall he died in a Canadian hospital in 1970.

Arthur Perkins
He came to work in Ambridge for a short time to replace the church windows. He married 'Mrs P' and took her back to London, but his health deteriorated and he went into a nursing home near Ambridge. He died in 1968.

Marianne Peters
She was an old flame of Paul Johnson, and turned up again in 1960 much to Christine's annoyance.

Jane Petrie
Jane ran the summer school at Arkwright Hall.

Amos Plant
'Mossy' Plant was, appropriately, in charge of Carol Tregorran's compost-grown vegetable business until he left in 1972.

Jim Price
Jim was the village postman and his wife, Ethel, was the postmistress in Ambridge for seventeen years. They retired to Cornwall in 1968, where Ethel later died.

George Randall
PC Randall served as Ambridge's village bobby for four years. He went back to Borchester on his promotion in 1955.

Dick Raymond
He was the district reporter of the *Borchester Echo* and the boy friend of Christine Archer at one time. He left when he got a job for a national newspaper in Fleet Street.

Paddy Redmond

Paddy Redmond was the handsome young Irishman who created havoc among the girls of Ambridge. He came to work for Dan Archer in 1965 and, although he was engaged to a girl back home in Ulster, he went out with several local lasses. He left hurriedly, not long after his fiancée, Nora McAuley, arrived from Ireland, and shortly before he was named as the father of Jennifer Archer's illegitimate child.

Thelma Rodgers

Mrs Rodgers, a widow, helped Jill Archer with her children for about three years until her husband changed jobs and they left the district in 1970.

Bill Sawyer

He was one-time chairman of the parish council and joined Walter Gabriel and Mrs Turvey in partnership in their pet shop. He retired in 1963 and moved to live in Borchester.

Mrs Scroby

She was well known locally as a freelance Mrs Mopp, but she too moved to Borchester in the sixties.

Lionel Quintus Shaw

He came to live in Ambridge after retiring as a company director, but wasn't happy in the country and moved back to the city life.

Bill Slater

Peggy Archer's cousin, he died after a fight at 'The Bull'. It was said at the inquest that he had a very thin skull, and a verdict of accidental death was recorded.

Tony Stobeman

He was a devil-may-care friend of Paul Johnson, and married Paul's sister, Sally. He opened a casino in

Borchester in partnership with Nelson Gabriel.

Len Thomas
A Welshman, he was shepherd to Dan Archer but eventually went back to Wales to start his own sheep farm after marrying Mary, a local girl.

Mrs Tonks
She ran for election to the Parish Council a couple of years ago and was successful. But then she went abroad before she could attend any of the meetings.

Roger Travers-Macy
Roger married Jennifer Archer and adopted her illegitimate child. He ran an antiquarian bookshop in Borchester, but gave it up when his marriage started breaking up. He is now a representative for a big company in Borchester.

Ellen Treadgold
She was Ralph Bellamy's housekeeper before he married. After the wedding, she decided to leave and find another position elsewhere.

Janet Tregorran
Janet was Ambridge's popular district nurse. She married John Tregorran, but was killed instantly in a car crash only four months after the wedding.

Sheila Trevelyan
She descended on Ambridge to write a book, which she did. She called it *Glasshouse Village* and was disappointed when she returned later, to find that no one in the village had read it, or knew she had been nasty about them.

Zebedee Tring
Zebedee was one of the village characters. He had been

farmhand and roadman around the district for many years, but was found dead in his cottage in 1973.

Minnie Waters
Minnie was one of the least glamorous barmaids at 'The Bull'. She left in 1966.

Fiona Watson
Fiona was Ambridge's 'Bo-Peep' – the highly-efficient herd-manager for Ralph Bellamy. She married and left in 1967.

David West
He came from Borchester and worked part-time in Fairbrothers Farm and part-time in the factory. He left in the fifties.

Godfrey Winstanley
Brigadier Winstanley, one of Ambridge's biggest land-owners and, for a short time, squire, was killed in a riding accident while out with the hunt. He had been a dour, stiff man who was very much bound by tradition. His military bearing made him a formidable-looking man, and his sharp tongue reinforced that impression.